SERGEI KOUSSEVITZKY — 1926

SERGEI KOUSSEVITZKY
AND HIS EPOCH

A BIOGRAPHICAL CHRONICLE

BY

ARTHUR LOURIÉ

TRANSLATED FROM THE RUSSIAN
BY S. W. PRING

Select Bibliographies Reprint Series

BOOKS FOR LIBRARIES PRESS
FREEPORT, NEW YORK

First Published 1931
Reprinted 1969

STANDARD BOOK NUMBER:
8369-5050-X

LIBRARY OF CONGRESS CATALOG CARD NUMBER:
78-94276

PRINTED IN THE UNITED STATES OF AMERICA

TO

NATALYA KONSTANTINOVNA KOUSSEVITZKY

If these words of Dostoevsky's are true of life —
and how true they are still! — the more certainly they
are true of art. What is the life of an artist, and what
is it called upon to serve? Particularly, is an artist
constrained by his vocation to be an intermediate link
between men and art? If we take this to be his allotted
destiny, his supreme task, his glorious exploit, his
ideal service, with all the ensuing consequences, what
more can we add to Dostoevsky's assertion? Everything is contained in it, as in a simple and elementary
formula. Always, in all times, it has been so. Of
course there are occasions when this material satisfaction of the spiritual hunger — a satisfaction which
appears to be a normal and fundamental need of men
in their relation to art — is eclipsed and replaced by
something else, by certain artificial demands, complex and abstract. Such eclipses occur from time to
time, when one great period in art gives way to another. They usually happen at the very moment when
the change takes place, when one era has departed
into the past and its successor has not yet matured,
has not expressed itself clearly, precisely, and con-
vincingly. The eclipse of the simple, substantial truths

does not usually last long, and vanishes like the mist as soon as the sun of the new epoch rises high enough to illuminate the freshly ploughed and sown fields. Under the vivifying rays the weeds of sophistry, æsthetic heresy, and perversion wither of themselves and disappear for a long while. Favourable conditions for the outbreak of a new artistic heresy and pseudo-creative devices do not present themselves until such time as the contemporary period passes into history, and just when the change — usually a painful one — occurs and the old is being superseded by the new. And so it is always — one cycle is completed and another begins. These three stages — the heritage of the past, the rupture and the seekings originated at the time of the change, and the conquests born of the newly-created culture — make up the whole life and activity of the artist. Of one such life in the conditions of our time I want to tell you.

TABLE OF CONTENTS

TABLE OF CONTENTS

LIST OF ILLUSTRATIONS

LIST OF ILLUSTRATIONS

PART I

CHAPTER ONE

A Portrait

THE WHOLE OF SERGEI KOUSSEVITZKY'S LIFE BEARS
the impress of one single passion — his ardent love
for music — which consumes his being as with fire.

A sharp distinction must be drawn between the
love of an artist for his profession — the normal love
of that for which he has a vocation — and the love of
which we are speaking. Every artist who gives himself up entirely to some branch of art has, of course,
and cannot help having, a love for it.

This is undoubtedly true, but the love which binds Koussevitzky to music is of an altogether different order. His relations with music have never been of the legitimate, normally established, professional type; all his life he has been her infatuated and clandestine lover. He is enamoured of his music with an ardour that nothing has ever quenched, and to this day the strength and vitality of his passion remain unimpaired. The vehemence, folly, and audacity of youth may have been replaced by wisdom and experience, but the flame of love burns as strongly as at any time, and will, I think, continue to do so as long as life endures.

Koussevitzky, the eternally youthful and insatiable lover of music, has become her lawful spouse — and in this is the key to the comprehension of himself and his activities. His art has been capricious and self-willed; it has not submitted to the established traditions and the rules of behaviour laid down for conductors. It has often been, and at times still is, at variance with them, preferring to act on independent and individual lines.

To me his conduct as an artist is most interesting

when it is at cross purposes with the normal and usual, when it transgresses the bounds of the generally recognized and normalized decorum; far more so than when it complies with the conventions, joins the professional front, and comes into line with the foremost conductors of the day, the men of outstanding merit, amongst whom he is by universal consent officially included. This general estimate of him, officially established, and widely admitted by the musical press and public, has little interest for me. Among conductor shares on the musical exchange Koussevitzky's are quoted high. His name, side by side with the best, represents the nth number of aces in the musical pack, and I am not in the least concerned as to which of these aces occupies the first place and which the last. It is entirely conditional. If you and I are playing musical bridge, the ace of trumps depends on the suit declaration. But let us not forget that the ace becomes a trump thanks entirely to the cards which support it, and apart from them is in an awkward situation; therefore the most musical form of musical bridge is always played without trumps.

One result of Koussevitzky's boundless enthusiasm for music is that he has always rushed at any new thing, no matter how unexpected and paradoxical the form it assumes. Directly a new musical spring is discovered, he draws from it to assuage his continual musical thirst. He can never have enough of it, and only when the waters prove to be poisonous, bitter, or simply insipid does he abandon them, and then apparently with regret.

Koussevitzky belongs to that category of musical enthusiasts of whom the imaginative literature of music tells us and of whom the professional musical practice of today knows least of all. Such enthusiasts are encountered in E. T. A. Hoffmann's gallery of heroes. They have an affinity with Kreisler, the mad kapellmeister, their ancestor, and from him they trace their genealogy, and not from the formal traditions and canons of any professional school of conductors, whoever its founder may have been and whoever its head — whether Bülow, Mahler, or Nikisch.

For those who thus love music it becomes the fundamental and supreme meaning of existence. They are organic musicians, and for them nothing can take the place of music. There are others for whom it is a superior handicraft, merely a "sensible business," and they find the fundamental and supreme meaning of life in something else, which often has nothing in common with music. Musicians belonging to the first category are almost beyond their profession; for them the centre of gravity in music lies outside its professional zone. If you begin to talk to them about professional questions of technique and craftsmanship, they will answer you absent-mindedly. These men are possessed by music as by an element.

Musicians of the second category are professional through and through, because they are connected with music only by their profession. Technically they are armed to the teeth. For them the outward forms are the most important thing in music. To the musical element they are often frankly hostile, since its intrusion always disturbs their calculations and constructions. Even if they are not hostile, they are indifferent, and many simply do not believe in its existence. In their practice they are aware, not of an ungovernable musical element, but only of the gentle

ripples on the surface of the tonal wave; the depths
of the element itself, the abysses of its chaos, are
unknown to them.

The romantics of the last century belonged to
the first category, and their ranks are steadily thin-
ning, whereas the cadres of the second category are
constantly being augmented. The numerical superiority of the latter at the present day is explained by
the fact that they strive at all costs to be in complete
accord with the spirit of the times — to bring culture
and art into conformity with the principles governing
the organization of modern life.

Koussevitzky is also included in the first category and has no place in the second. At certain moments he may be found with the latter, but simply
through weakness and misapprehension, when he
wants to be in harmony with his period. He is among
them only as a stranger and a guest. Essentially he
has no contact with the objectively impersonal tendencies of contemporary music, which applies itself to
the formal, constructional, and organizational side
of the art. His place is among the solitaries — the
romantics, the fantasts, and the visionaries. . . .

Here he is himself, at home, surrounded by his own people.

I think it is entirely purposeless to argue as to which is the better, which the worse. We have to reckon with the fact that both kinds of musicians exist. The only question is whether they do good or bad work in connexion with the category to which they belong. It is impossible, for the sake of an abstract principle, to suppress some by others, to destroy one thing in order to affirm another. Every artistic phenomenon should be subject to appraisement as an individual fact, in its individual significance, apart from the general propositions put forward by the conditions of the moment or period, since these propositions, taken as abstract principles, are powerless to augment or diminish anything in respect of art. It is, perhaps, the chief thing we learn from the experience gained when one tendency in art gives way to another. All the rest is, of course, elucidated from the observation of particular cases and the investigation of details.

This division of musicians (whether composers or performers) into two camps is still very sharply defined, notwithstanding that it has become thoroughly irksome, and that the strife between them has lasted for more than a decade. It reminds one of the dissensions in the middle of last century between the adherents of the so-called program music and the supporters of pure music, when Hanslick proclaimed his theory of the " musically beautiful." It is essentially almost the same thing over again, but in the conditions of a new time and a new culture. The difference is only in the terms used, in the fact that these tendencies are now called individualism and collectivism respectively. We have again two artistic outlooks opposed to each other — two hostile and irreconcilable worlds, existing simultaneously and repudiating each other. And both tendencies are the living reflection of the times; taken together, they express the contemporary dualism, which defines our contemporary æsthetic as such in its entirety.

Koussevitzky is not a professional in the sense in which the term is understood today, when professionalism is regarded as a self-sufficing technique, an object in itself and not a means to an end; in this sense he is not a professional virtuoso of the orchestra.

His professionalism is hardly perceptible in his conducting; with him it occupies the lowest place, and plays a merely menial, subsidiary part, always subordinated to life and the interpretation. It is of the same order as that of a man who walks, eats, drinks, laughs, and weeps, never reflecting on what he is doing.

An exceptionally emotional pathos underlies Koussevitzky's orchestral conducting. To him it is everything. The professional and technical side of the business is reduced to extracting the emotional pathos from the work he is playing and, in direct contact with the listener, communicating it to him. The quality, power, and convincingness of the performance depend solely on the emotional element which he obtains from the music and imparts to the audience. The less emotional fire there is in the music, the greater will be the resistance of the latter to his conducting; and, conversely, the more a musical composition is saturated with feeling, the more easily will it submit itself to him, and here he will prove to be in his own sphere.

A passionate, sensuous love of music, and the ability to feel, to experience, the music he is performing, are combined in him. With him the one quality

*"With pain I always shall remember
The unproductive land of Tver."*

(AKHMATOVA)

CHAPTER TWO

Childhood

SERGEI ALEXANDROVITCH KOUSSEVITZKY WAS BORN
on 13/26 June 1874 at Vyshny Volochek, a poor little
town, now hardly discoverable on the map, situated in
the Tver Government, which forms part of the central
zone of Russia. Vyshny Volochek is in no way remarkable, and its small population of a few thousands
are submerged in the monotonous, everyday existence
characteristic of such a place. A drab, wearisome life,
in which nothing changes and one day is as like

another as two peas; the years spent in it flash past like
the milestones on the highway. A place where every
trifling incident assumes enormous importance and is
debated in every key; where life is full of trivial cares
and petty emotions. A place which the ripples of the
world-wave never reach; where everything is always
at a standstill, and nothing ever happens; where events
occurring in the great cities present themselves to the
inhabitants as fantastic and are with difficulty com-
prehended by them. Where the noises of the music of
the world — the vast human life — seem to be merely
a dream. . . . How many towns like it are scattered
over the huge expanse of the Russian land! And in
America! And in Europe! Now, if only a little place
such as Vyshny Volochek has the good fortune to become the cradle of a visionary, an artist, a savant, or
even of an architect of life, its name will be rescued
from obscurity, and will appear in all the diction-
aries. In bygone times it would have been the subject
of engravings, and today pictures of it will be shown
on the cinema screen. Such a town is lucky if it is
destined to be the birthplace ˙of someone who will
enter into the world-family. In this is its only hope,

and the justification for the long years of a sterile and monotonous existence. . . . In what does the justification consist? Surely not in the fact that the inhabitants may be puffed up with pride in their celebrated fellow-townsman, to whose birthplace they have affixed a tablet after his decease or, in the best instance, have erected an abominable memorial on its only square, where, defiled by the pigeons, in the early morning it will be the eternal and immovable witness of the fishwives' daily squabbles; through the day will be the referee of the games of the youngsters returning home from school; and in the evening twilight will be compelled, resignedly and involuntarily, to overhear the foolish and sensual whispers and babblings of a pair of lovers who have taken refuge on the nearest bench. . . . There you have the fundamental features of what is called posthumous fame.

No, the justification is not in this, but in the fact that when the man goes out into the wide expanse of life, he will as long as he lives remember his home, that little bit of soil where he first saw the light of day. He will always be nourished on the juices of the land which fed him, and, recollecting that land in his creative work and in his consciousness, no matter what form his activity takes, he will transmute the life which fills the scrap of his native soil, making it — that life — radiant and purified. The recollection will always be tender and precious to him; and the more notable his activities become, the greater will be the transformation in his creative work.

The humdrum daily life of the simple, ordinary people amidst whom the man was born and grew up, having ceased to impede and fetter him in his aspiration for space and his longing actively and brilliantly to manifest his individuality, acquires another meaning, the meaning of a life of peace and simplicity, and all that has been accumulated and preserved in the memories of childhood and the years of his early youth will for ever be a precious treasure, will be vital nutriment producing creative fruit. This is the substratum in which are found the deepest and most intimate roots.

Koussevitzky has always preserved a vivid recollection of his home-places. He is an ardent lover of his native land, and the ties with it have bound him with living fetters at the various periods of his life.

This attitude towards it has always helped him to bear up against obstacles which have often been very serious and distressing, since "nobody is a prophet in his own country." Koussevitzky's birthplace, the Tver country, has the typical landscape of the central Russian zone — melancholy, monotonous, meagre. A sorrowful land, rugged and poverty-stricken, but lovely, permeated with a tender beauty, like the folk-song of these places. In the summer the breeze sweeps over the fields sown with rye; the fields whose wide expanse is filled with the music of nature, in which the song of the lark blends naturally with the voices of the haymakers and harvesters. In the winter the snowy covering, sparkling like a dazzling shroud, reveals endless distances and vast horizons, edged by a slender line on which, as though in Indian ink, are etched the birch groves, the fir forests. . . .

The boy was born in a poor family, a family unknown to anyone, but a musical family. Music was partly a means of earning the daily bread, partly a respite from the worries of life, a consolation amid its misfortunes. The father gave lessons on the violin for a paltry fee, the mother played the piano. In the evening the father, wearied of his day's work, got out the wretched fiddle, and the boy, tucked away in the corner, listened eagerly to the dismal and pitiful sounds which spoke artlessly of a sorry fate, of a distressful life in which there was no glimmer of light, of dreams that were never realized, of the native land, of its forests and groves and boundless fields. . . . His father's music was the original source of the sounds which Koussevitzky drank in during the first years of his life. His mother died when the child was three years old.

He was left an orphan, left to himself and to that unknown future which fate was preparing for him. His father could not look after his son's upbringing, owing to ignorance and lack of means. The boy grew up like the grass of the field, listening to the voices of nature and to himself, guided solely by his instincts, which began to stir in him early and became the prime, if not the only, mover in his development. The main, fundamental instinct defined itself at once as a passionate fondness for musical sounds. The love of music was the first feeling which grew up persistently in the boy's soul. Of his own accord he gradually learnt to play every instrument, his principal teachers at that time being the strolling musicians, wandering from place to place, from one village to another. . . . Sometimes Serge followed them, often escaping from home for several days, turning himself into a little vagrant, attracted as though hypnotized by the enchantment, irresistible to him, of the sounds which the itinerants extracted from their instruments.

Another very powerful source was a pronounced love of nature, which possessed him from early childhood. A need of solitude was created in the boy. He went off into the forest and spent whole days there, listening to the mysterious voices of nature and the vague but compelling summons which began to resound in his soul. To this period of his childhood belong the earliest attempts at musical composition. A small, typically provincial theatre was opened in the town. Classical dramas and tragedies were given, *Kean, Hamlet,* and *Richard III* being the mainstay of the repertory. Music was required for the entr'actes, and who was to arrange it if not the boy, for whom it provided a possibility of testing his powers and displaying the " knowledge " he had acquired? The composition of this "music" at the same time provided young Serge with his first lessons in musical dictation, since it was written from the singing voice.

In every corner of Russia some form of culture and enlightenment has always existed. The germ of this may be someone whom fate has flung into the more-dead-than-alive provinces, but nearly always you may come upon a lonely figure standing out prominently on the grey background of provincial life.

Vyshny Volochek provided a typical instance in the family of an engineer named Ropenberg, whose official duties obliged him to reside in the little town. After his death the widow stayed on with her little daughter. Maria Fedorovna Ropenberg was still a young woman; cultured and well educated, she was also a fine pianist, a pupil of Nikolai Rubinstein. When he was eight years old, Serge struck up a friendship with the little girl, who became the playmate of his childhood. Her mother took notice of the vivacious, contemplative boy who displayed a passionate love of music, and she occupied herself seriously with his education. It was she who first introduced him to the classics — Bach, Mozart, Beethoven — whose compositions she played to him. She gave Serge lessons on the piano, and under her tuition he made such progress that he began to play duets with her.

Madame Ropenberg's influence was an exceptionally fortunate happening in Serge's childhood. In addition to providing him with his first professional musical training she treated the boy, who had not known a mother's care, with particular tenderness and solicitude. Koussevitzky always remembers with heart-felt emotion and gratitude this kindly, sensitive woman, who afterwards witnessed the musical achievements of her foster-child and pupil and saw with pride the fruits of the seed sown by her.

The theatrical experiments, too, had not been in vain: the Vyshny Volochek theatre initiated starring tours in the principal town in the Government, Tver, and took Serge with them to look after the musical department. Between the ages of twelve and fourteen he did all the musical work in connexion with these tours.

He became conductor of the primitive little orchestra, which played in the intervals at every performance. The little conductor was enthusiastically appreciated by the "bearded" musicians, who made much of him.

Hence began Koussevitzky's close connexion with the theatrical world, and later, in the first period of his life in Moscow, his nearest friends were almost always actors. At one time he seriously contemplated adopting the stage as a profession.

His first appearances as a conductor were not in the nature of a joke, but were important events in Serge's life: after them the idea of continuing his present existence grew more and more impossible. It became clear to him that if he wished to follow a musical career, serious study was indispensable. Vyshny Volochek was too circumscribed for him. To remain longer in such unenlightened surroundings meant the abandonment of all his hopes and threatened with ruin and disaster all his childish visions. But how were the yearning for serious training, the desire to emerge on to the broad highway of life — how were they to be realized?

In the social conditions with which his life was encompassed they could be nothing more than a dream. His father, a man of the old school, bound by tradition and worn out by the struggle for existence, did not understand his son's aspirations. Nor did he sympathize with the latter's proposal to become a professional musician — it is doubtful whether he even took into consideration what was implied by the term. He desired for his son a sounder and more practical career. Serge's dreams clashed with his father's distinct and determined opposition; the latter was inflexible and would not listen to any talk of a serious musical training for the boy — a training, moreover, which was to be carried out away from home, in the far-off capital. Again, the family had no resources wherewith to finance these plans. It seemed to them the foolhardiness and wayward caprice of a self-confident youngster. He would have to come to a firm decision, to break with his family and go his own way, at the mercy of fate. Flight was the only solution. Making a bundle of his more than modest belongings, one bright day, which seemed to him more propitious for his venture, the boy left the house secretly, with three roubles in his pocket, gripped with a feeling of anguish as he thought of the rupture with his people, but with his heart filled with a

---

"Moscow, Moscow . . ."

(PUSHKIN)

CHAPTER THREE

Student Years

A᙮ THAT TIME THE TWO MOST IMPORTANT INSTITU-
tions in Moscow for the training of professional musicians were the Conservatory and the Philharmonic
School. Serge hurried to the former, but was completely unsuccessful. The Director, V. I. Safonov,
pianist and conductor, categorically refused even to
permit him to sit for examination, in view of the fact
that the term had already begun. The refusal was
decisive and formal.

In compliance with the general conditions laid down for the admission of new students, Koussevitzky would have to wait till the spring — that is, to lose a year's teaching — which would have been madness. He therefore turned to the Philharmonic, but here a similar fate awaited him. The Director, Shestakovsky, displayed the same formal and impersonal attitude. " You've come too late; all the vacancies are filled," he said. " I'm very sorry, but you'll have to wait till next year."

The second failure greatly perturbed the boy, and he vented his feelings in a spirited and rebellious protest. The tears welled up into his eyes, his heart began to throb furiously, and with despair in his voice he exclaimed: "I can't wait . . . I don't want to wait . . . I want to study; I must, I will study . . . I won't go away. You dare not drive me away. . . . You must help me. Give me a chance to study."

The scene in the private room between the boy and the Director had a decisive effect. The aged musician was touched, and the formalism of the administrator and director gave way to the sympathy of the artist. In the words of rebellion and protest, in the passionate agitation of the boy, Shestakovsky perceived something more than mere persistence and obstinacy. He felt that this was an instance of a genuine vocation, he saw that he had to do with an exceptional phenomenon, and — well, in such a case it was quite permissible to infringe the rules by which everybody was governed. Shestakovsky soothed the boy. " Calm yourself, my boy," he said. " There's no need to be so upset. . . . Everything shall be arranged. We'll make it possible for you to study. We'll test your abilities at once; and if they prove satisfactory, you shall be admitted to the school."

The examination took place then and there and revealed fine qualifications — more than were needed to pass him in — an absolute ear and an excellent musical memory. Serge breathed easily — the vision of a musical training had become a reality. All he had to do now was to choose a subject in which to specialize.

The boy had already dreamed of conducting — to become the conductor of an orchestra seemed to him the height of bliss — but on first entering the school it was impossible even to think of it, let alone mention it.

At that time there was no class for instruction in the art of conducting. As he not merely was unable to pay for lessons, but also lacked the means of subsistence, the little musician's choice of a special subject was limited to three instruments, the study of which was free and furthermore included a small bursary, which would help him to live. These bursaries had already been allotted at the Philharmonic, and at this period of the term there were only three still vacant — the horn, the trombone, and the double-bass. The wind-instruments did not appeal to Serge, and he chose the double-bass. This instrument, which was held in utter contempt by the students, in which nobody was interested, and which was regarded as occupying the lowliest place in the orchestra, attracted him just because it was neglected — unfairly, as he thought — and because the boy had a vague feeling that it held new, hitherto unexploited possibilities of development. Moreover, when all was said and done, it was a stringed instrument — very harsh, it was true, and almost embarrassing, but nevertheless directly related to the noble family of the string quartet.

And so the choice was made. Without delay they brought a double-bass into Shestakovsky's private room and "tried it on" the new pupil, to see if it fitted his height and his hands. As a matter of fact, Serge was hardly half as big as his fiddle, and this was rather disconcerting, but Professor Rambausek examined his hands and found them exceptionally suitable for playing a stringed instrument.

Thus, by a strange and unexpected concourse of circumstances, Serge became a double-bass player, a specialty which had never entered into his mind, but which he was destined ultimately to raise to a level entirely unknown at this time, a pitch of perfection lost by this instrument since the days of two remarkable virtuosi of the nineteenth century — the Italians Dragonetti and Bottesini.

The double-bass class was one of the least important in the Philharmonic School. It was taught by Professor Rambausek, a musician of education and culture, who had a few students, for the most part preparing to fill the orchestral ranks of the future. In this class the new pupil soon occupied the first place among his comrades by reason of his exceptional skill in overcoming difficulties, and his extraordinary zeal and energy. The preparatory work on which he had spent considerable time before entering the Philharmonic proved to be so substantial that the boy strode along in seven-league boots, far outstripping the period fixed for the completion of the course. Rambausek became very fond of Serge and was as attached to him as if he were his own son. The Professor's family took the place of the one which the boy had forsaken. Rambausek surrounded him with an atmosphere of consideration, kindness, and affection. Making unusually rapid progress, in five months Serge completed under his guidance a course for which five years were allowed. The enthusiastic Rambausek arranged to bring him out at a pupils' concert. This was the first occasion in the history of a Russian conservatory of a student's début in the quality of a virtuoso on the double-bass.

Serge attracted attention and began to be talked about, at first within the walls of the school and then

SERGEI KOUSSEVITZKY
at the age of 15, as Student of the Moscow Conservatory

farther afield. His performances on so huge and primitive an instrument seemed to be something altogether unusual, and his fellow-students who were learning other instruments began to turn to him for advice on questions of technique and execution. This was the beginning of his intercourse with the future musicians of the orchestra, and of the development of an independent attitude towards the interpretation of musical compositions. Simultaneously with his study of the double-bass Koussevitzky took the course in the theory of music, which was compulsory at the Conservatory and the Philharmonic. He studied harmony with S. Kruglikov, and counterpoint and free composition with the famous operatic composer and teacher of that time, Blaremberg.

In his seventeenth year Serge, still a Philharmonic student, was admitted to the orchestra of the Imperial Theatre without a contest. At first he occupied the lowest place in the ranks, but at the end of a year became the leader of the double-basses. He made it a condition that he should have the right to the title of soloist, which in those days did not exist for the orchestral double-bass.

In 1894 he completed his studies and graduated from the Philharmonic Conservatory.

The scholastic period ended, independent artistic activity began. About this time he was concerned in an amusing incident, which can only be described as boyish mischief, but which testifies to his mastery of the double-bass.

In St. Petersburg a competition was announced, to fill the vacant post of leader of the double-basses at the Imperial Opera. The competition committee consisted of Napravnik, Auer, Verzhbilovich, and others. Koussevitzky had only just gained an excellent footing in Moscow as an orchestral soloist; he was very well satisfied with this position and had no intention of resigning it in exchange for another. By way of a joke, and with the purpose of testing his powers and proving himself, he announced his desire to participate in the St. Petersburg competition, and put in an appearance for the contest. His coming forward caused a sensation. The members of the committee had not even suspected the possibility of such technique on the double-bass, nor the quality of tone which Koussevitzky revealed to them. They expressed them-

occupied a lowly place in the orchestra and had been considered as almost on a level with the instruments of percussion; that he had given it a serious significance and shown new possibilities of playing on it. He longed for more. He aimed at the impossible. An artistic temperament and ambition drove him to it, in order to make this instrument — harsh and primitive according to general opinion — of equal importance with the violin or the 'cello. He wanted to put it in the front rank of solo concert instruments, and, paradoxical though it may seem, he accomplished his purpose. With even greater zeal than before he worked at its technique and attained an altogether exceptional virtuosity, refining the expression and intonation of the double-bass to such a degree that it was hardly distinguishable from the 'cello. On his hearers it produced a stupefying impression. Koussevitzky achieved celebrity; he became the vogue. The Moscow salons vied with one another in their efforts to capture this strange young man who played a huge and clumsy monstrosity of an instrument as though he had beneath his fingers the fragile and feminine 'cello. The fame of his performances spread beyond the confines

SERGEI KOUSSEVITZKY
as Virtuoso on the Double-bass; in 1906

of Moscow and St. Petersburg. He toured Russia as a double-bass concert soloist and finally went abroad, to western Europe.

In 1898 he made his first appearance in Berlin, at the Singakademie. His recollections of the concert are interesting. The agency to whom he entrusted his arrangements regarded him as the usual foreign star. Having obtained the customary fee from him, they fixed up a concert, but not a single poster was to be seen in the city. When Koussevitzky expressed his misgivings on the subject, they replied: " You're surprised that there aren't any posters? You're a strange man! Why do you want them? Nobody knows you here, so who would read them? " The young man was indignant. " What do you mean by ' Who would read them? ' " he demanded. " I should read them myself."

Since the triumphant appearances of Anton Rubinstein and Davydov, the 'cellist, no Russian artist had performed before a foreign audience. There had been an interregnum, during which the Russians were forgotten. It was not until the beginning of the new century that the westward movement of Russian artists began. Koussevitzky was one of the first. We have just had an instance of the scepticism in regard to him. Loewenfeld, Director of the Schiller Theatre, to whom he had letters of introduction, organized a reception for him, to which representatives of the Berlin musical world were invited. Koussevitzky played the bass. In this way the ground was prepared for his concert at the Singakademie.

After the Berlin concert, which had a great success, the attitude towards him underwent a change. Posters were put up and proposals for other concerts were made. In 1900 Koussevitzky was invited to Düsseldorf, to play the double-bass part in Bach's *Phœbus and Pan,* under the baton of Richard Strauss. This was the first meeting of the future conductor with the modernist composer.

The development of his career as a double-bass virtuoso soloist in Russia and abroad compelled him seriously to turn his thoughts to his repertory. There was hardly anything for solo performance on his instrument. The 'cello pieces of Popper and Bruch were in great vogue at that time, especially the latter's *Kol Nidrei.* These Koussevitzky transposed for the double-bass, and they formed the pièces de résistance of his programs. Having played through everything that was available, he was obliged to create a literature himself. In 1900 he set to work to write and transpose music for his instrument. Here is a list of what was accomplished at that time:

Transcriptions

1. Handel . . . . Sonata for violin
2. Galliard . . . . . . Sonata for 'cello
3. Eccles. . . . . Sonata for 'cello
4. Mozart . . . . Concerto for bassoon fiddle
5. Bruch . . . . *Kol Nidrei*
6. Bach . . . . Aria from Cantata No. 12
7. R. Strauss. . . . . Sonata for 'cello
8. A. Scriabin. . . . Two Études, op. 74

and much else from compositions by various composers for different instruments.

Four pieces written by Koussevitzky for the double-bass belong to this period. They are:

1. *Valse miniature*
2. *Chanson triste*
3. *Andante*
4. *Humoresque*

In 1902 he composed a concerto for double-bass and orchestra. His compositions for the instrument serve to supplement the very scanty literature at its disposal.

It is interesting to note that the three remarkable double-bass virtuosi — Dragonetti, Bottesini, and Koussevitzky — are separated from one another by intervals of fifty years. It is as though musical culture could not permit itself the luxury of more than two double-bass soloists in one century.

The two Italians — Dragonetti and Bottesini — were at the same time conductors. The development of double-bass playing and the mastering and enriching of the technical and tonal possibilities of the instrument are connected for nearly a century and a half with the names of these three musicians.

Dragonetti appears to have been the earliest virtuoso of the double-bass. He was contemporary with Beethoven, who was enraptured with Dragonetti's technique, and under the influence of his playing wrote the double-bass recitative in the Ninth Symphony, and the double-bass part in the scherzo of the Fifth. When Koussevitzky began his career as a double-bass soloist, the memory of Bottesini was still green. Koussevitzky's playing, in comparison with his predecessors', was modernized; he toned down and really transformed the typical sonority of the orchestral bass, approximating it to that of the 'cello. He gave us none of the straight-line contours and simplified intonations characteristic of this type of instrument. Like his orchestral interpretations, his playing was refined, exquisite, and expressive.

CHAPTER FOUR

A Serenade on the Double-Bass

In KOUSSEVITZKY'S BIOGRAPHY THERE ARE NO TRAGIC shades. Not only that — in it there is nothing that suggests misfortune, domestic or external. Fate has always been kind to him; from the very beginning of his artistic career down to the present day everything has gone smoothly and happily. If there have been upsets, they have always been of a general and not of a personal nature, changing not only his life, but the lives of all around him, as in the years of the war and the revolution. Such an absence of the dramatic, such an even flow of events, in which the equilibrium is always maintained, appears to be very rare, if not unprecedented, in the life of an artist, whatever his sphere. Confronted with this, one hardly knows which way to turn. One becomes doubtful. One writes a biography and suddenly perceives that there is essentially no biography. . . . There is a steady succession of events or facts of greater or less importance, which follow one another according to rule. Anything that might in any way check that even flow is sternly eliminated from the life of the subject of the biography. Anything that might rouse him to opposition or irritate him is kept away from him, and thus strife is avoided and tranquillity secured. The very best conditions for the development of the artist's activities are consciously and persistently created. Such conditions have endured with amazing constancy during Koussevitzky's career as a conductor, which has now extended over a period of twenty-five years.

I think that if he had been a creative artist, so much good fortune would have been disastrous to him and would have destroyed his powers of creation. As a performer he found these conditions of life ideal for the expansion of his talents.

What is the clue to the explanation of such a destiny? It is quite simple. Here a woman, a friend, a wife, plays her part.

Natalya Konstantinovna Koussevitzkaya has too great a share in her husband's life to permit of our speaking of him without mentioning her. This woman's love is the key to the comprehension of the exceptionally favourable circumstances attending his career as a conductor and all his other activities. Koussevitzky himself was subject to the changes of mood and fits of disenchantment and vacillation which are natural to every artist and every man. Upon Natalya Konstantinovna devolved the duty of maintaining his demeanour in the affairs of life at an even temperature. Like a sentry she was always on guard for his peace and comfort, his happiness, his progress and success. It may be imagined that she invariably took upon herself everything of a burdensome, unpleasant, hostile nature, so that when it reached him, it had been rendered harmless. The cruder aspects of life's happenings she faced herself, and he was not allowed to see them until they had been reduced to order and become tractable and pleasing. . . . Without her intervention it is difficult even to conceive what his life would have been. There can be no doubt that it would have had an altogether different meaning and would have assumed other contours. Without exaggeration, it may almost be said that Natalya Konstantinovna was her husband's Providence.

This woman's extraordinary abilities, great intellectual powers, exceptional strength of will, power of influence, and confidence in regard to life and men — all this taken together she brought as an offering to the idol of her affections, instead of asserting herself and using it for her personal advantage. She compelled herself to serve that idol whole-heartedly and with boundless self-denial. She became, as it were, blind and deaf to everything save her feelings for her husband and her devotion to his artistic career. At the same time she concealed from the eyes of the world the role she had assumed, effacing herself to the last degree, locking herself up in silence, almost annihilating herself. . . . In her, two traits are strangely blended — an all but consuming energy, indomitable persistence and obstinacy in regard to everything that concerns her husband, but in everything that affects herself gentleness and extraordinary modesty, almost amounting to bashfulness. . . . Such are the general characteristics of the woman who in 1901 entered into Koussevitzky's life and played a decisive part in it.

From the moment of her meeting with Koussevitzky, Natalya Konstantinovna took a most vital and active interest in all his achievements, plans, aspirations, projects for the future, everything, assisting her husband with energy and determination. From that moment Koussevitzky in conjunction with his wife made his career as a conductor a reality. It became, so to speak, the creative work of Natalya Konstantinovna's life, her chef-d'œuvre, a substitute for her own artistic efforts at sculpture, at which, prior to her meeting with him, she had worked with enthusiasm and which she sacrificed to her husband, on a par with everything else that she did for him.

In the person of Natalya Konstantinovna, Koussevitzky found an ideal helper and friend, who made it possible for him to realize everything for which he had consciously and unconsciously striven and which would have come to naught unless conditions so favourable for it had been created.

The twenty-fifth anniversary of his conductorship was the silver jubilee not only of his work as an artist, but also of his marriage with his faithful and devoted wife, with whom he has gone through the years.

1901 arrived. . . . The days followed one another in measured succession. Koussevitzky spent the winter in Moscow, dividing his time between work at the theatre and lessons at the Philharmonic. In the evenings he attended social gatherings, where he astonished his audiences by his double-bass playing. From time to time he appeared at concerts. At one such evening, when he came on to the platform, he saw in the front row, quite near to him, almost at his feet, a fair stranger, who listened to him with eager attention. Their eyes met and it seemed to him as though he had been scorched by a lightning-flash. He felt that something significant had come into his life. An inner feeling whispered to him that this meeting was fraught with destiny and would change his whole existence. Nor was he mistaken, for so it fell out. A line of demarcation was drawn, dividing his past life from that which began from this moment. It was not until 1905 that Natalya Ushkova became Koussevitzky's wife.

Two years elapsed from the time of their first meeting before Koussevitzky discovered the name of his " fair unknown." Since that memorable day he had sought her everywhere, but had not found her. After long months of torment and fruitless quests they met again for a moment in a brilliantly lighted concert hall, surrounded by a noisy crowd, separated by the platform as by a fatal barrier. On such an occasion everything he played was transformed into a serenade on the double-bass, intended for her alone amidst an indifferent throng. Then they lost sight of each other once more.

In the winter she went abroad, to Paris, where she studied social science at the school directed by the remarkable Russian savant Maxim Kovalevsky. The summer she spent with her relatives in the country. Filled with love and longing, he stared at every woman he met in the street; and when he entered a house, it was with nervous and trembling expectation, in the hope of finding her. . . .

At last they became acquainted. But it was some time before Natalya Ushkova obtained her own way and was able to form a friendship with the artist. She was of an independent nature, but belonged to a very different social circle from his and had grown up in a family steeped in tradition and fettered by prejudices and conventions. In 1905 the double-bass serenade with which Sergei Koussevitzky had for nearly five years enchanted the " fair unknown " came to an end, and Natalya Ushkova became his wife.

Simultaneously with the serenade Koussevitzky brought his career as a virtuoso of the double-bass to a close and began the realization of his project of becoming a conductor. He still continued to work at the bass and to appear as a soloist, but this ceased to be his principal aim and gradually receded into the background. The foreground was occupied almost exclusively by thoughts of wielding the conductor's baton. The chief impulse to this came from his disenchantment with his role as a virtuoso. He had exhausted the possibilities of the double-bass and could go no further in this direction. The position attained by him in this and subsequent years put him in the ranks of the foremost virtuosi. His name was mentioned on an equality with those of Kreisler and Casals. Meanwhile the musical energy and powers which he felt within himself not only were unexhausted, but seemed as though they had only just begun to expand. He could not and did not want to mark time, easy in his mind and contented with what he had achieved. To take up another instrument would have been absurd, and musical composition was not his vocation; there remained only one outlet for the extension of his musical activities — the path to the orchestral conductor's desk, of which he had dreamed and to which he had aspired since the days of his childhood.

CHAPTER FIVE

From Double-Bass to Conductor's Desk

KOUSSEVITZKY SETTLED IN BERLIN. HIS EXPERIENCE of conducting began in 1906 with the students' orchestra of the Berlin Hochschule, which Joachim permitted to be placed at his disposal.

This orchestra served him as a touchstone. To all intents and purposes the professional school of orchestral conducting was created at that time. Berlin and Leipzig were the headquarters; they produced a brilliant group of conductors at the beginning of the twentieth century and were inundated with young men desirous of following the profession.

The predominant position in the existing surroundings was occupied by Nikisch's class at Leipzig. An opinion has been prevalent that Koussevitzky was a member of Nikisch's class. This is not so. Koussevitzky did not study with any of the conductors who at that period were stars of the first magnitude. Like most of the prominent men in this sphere, he worked independently. He studied the technique of conducting exclusively from living examples. He attended the concerts of Nikisch, Mahler, Weingartner, Mottl, and Schuch and followed their performances from the score; this he regarded as equivalent to practical lessons. He watched and absorbed the methods employed by these virtuosi of the orchestra and at the same time evolved a technique of his own by means of an original system. Having learnt a score by heart, he made some pianist play it in accordance with the plan which he himself intended to adopt in conducting this composition. Whilst the pianist was playing, Koussevitzky conducted, and he had the work repeated until he had mastered the technique of the gestures necessary in the given instance. He devised this method for himself, not because he was not a pianist, but because it was for him the most convenient and practical.

When he had studied a composition sufficiently to have complete control of his gestures without the necessity of further supervision, he turned to the orchestra. This system of studying a score he has continued to the present day. Thanks to it he acquired that complete freedom in his movements and gestures which is essential to a conductor, and, most important, developed a plastic technique in his handling of the orchestra. Side by side with the convenience connected with it, this original method of learning a score caused not a little unpleasantness to Koussevitzky, particularly at the beginning of his career, and contributed to attacks on him (which, by the way, were very naïve). As though it mattered how a score was learnt — whether by eyes, ears, or fingers! The important thing is that it should be performed; the rest is of no consequence. The writing of music is analogous — is it not all one whether the composer does or does not make use of an instrument?

In former times a prejudice of this nature did

exist in regard to a composer. The admission that he wrote his music at an instrument seemed compromising and was considered a sign, if not of anti-musicality, at all events of a manifest helplessness. Nowadays that prejudice has lost its force, at least amongst cultured musicians. We know that composition away from the instrument adds nothing to the quality of the work. The method of composing with the aid of any instrument does not, of course, mean picking the music out with the fingers, which is not worth anything, but that concrete sensation of the material, without which no contemporary art exists.

If this does not exactly apply to the learning of a score, there is undoubtedly a certain analogy.

Koussevitzky made his début as a conductor in Berlin with the Philharmonic Orchestra on January 23, 1908. His first appearance, according to the recollections of those who were present, produced an impression of freshness, novelty, and power. The Berlin critics remarked that the big conductors would soon have to reckon with the entry into their ranks of a new, serious rival.

In subsequent seasons Koussevitzky came forward as an orchestral conductor in Berlin, London, Paris, and Vienna. In the last two cities his concerts at that time were only star appearances. His visits to Berlin and London were annual, and in these capitals his concerts began to be systematically planned.

From the very first, Koussevitzky made a point of including new musical compositions in his programs. This did not always work smoothly; at times he came up against the opposition of the orchestra. A certain persuasiveness and persistence on the part of the young conductor were necessary in order to overcome such opposition. An interesting case happened in London.

In 1910 Koussevitzky was invited to conduct a subscription concert of the London Symphony. He chose for his program Scriabin's *Poem of Ecstasy*. During the first rehearsal this work proved to be so extraordinary that the musicians assumed a manifestly hostile attitude towards it. Koussevitzky had to surmount the stubborn resistance of the orchestra, who rebelled at having to play such absurd stuff as this music seemed to them on a first reading. Enamoured of the score of the *Poem of Ecstasy*, which afterwards became one of the central works in his repertory, Koussevitzky put up a stubborn defence on its behalf. He declared that the revolt which he now perceived in their ranks would be transformed into enthusiasm within a year, and that they would be proud to think that they had first played it with him. His efforts were crowned with a success which surpassed his expectations. Even before the piece was performed at the concert, the orchestra hastened to tell him that he would not have to wait a year for their appreciation of the *Poem*. The work on it at the rehearsals had convinced them that he was right.

Koussevitzky's earliest appearances as a conductor marked the beginning of that resolute and persistent propaganda for new music which became one of the distinguishing features of his career.

For some time after he had become the conductor of an orchestra he did not relinquish his role as double-bass player. Despite the fact that he now attached less importance to the latter than to the former, these particular years were marked by his exceptionally brilliant performances as a soloist. He played in all the great European centres and undertook an extensive concert tour through Scandinavia. In Berlin he appeared at the Philharmonic under Nikisch, in Dresden under Schuch, in Paris under Colonne. Just about this time he took part in a concert at the Gewandhaus, Leipzig, conducted by Nikisch. There is an interesting story attached to this. Arthur Nikisch heard Koussevitzky on the double-bass in Russia; he was captivated, and invited him to play under him at the Gewandhaus. Koussevitzky was delighted and flattered, as such an invitation was considered a great honour for a young artist. But it was not officially endorsed. When Koussevitzky met Nikisch in Germany and reminded him of it, the latter was much disconcerted. He told Koussevitzky that the directors of the Gewandhaus had expressed themselves as opposed to the invitation, on the ground that the double-bass was not a classical instrument. Koussevitzky was stung to the quick. In reply he gave on his own initiative two concerts in Leipzig and displayed his mastery of the " non-classical " instrument. The directors attended them, and as a result they hastened to send him an official invitation to appear as a soloist. Thus was demolished the theory that the double-bass was not a classical instrument.

At that time the number of instrumental virtuosi was very limited, but they were undoubtedly of a better quality than nowadays, when the extraordinary over-production of virtuosity creates a very illusive impression.

In the sphere of technical attainments the average level has beyond a doubt been considerably raised, but at the expense of the individuality and independence of the virtuosi, of whom the vast majority have adapted themselves to the demands of the crowd. Most of them, in every department of music, demolish the purely artistic bases of musical culture and cheapen their art in proportion as the process of collectivization develops, and the masses who held aloof from music draw closer and closer to it and become almost its chief patrons, as is now the case. In the aristocratic periods of musical history matters were otherwise, but as soon as democracy gathered round the musical platform and proclaimed authoritative rights over musical production and consumption, radical changes took place.

Koussevitzky's virtuoso activities appear to be atavistic — a reversion to the type of the aristocratic musical cultures — and to a considerable extent this may also be said of his activities as a conductor.

But to his double-bass virtuosity this applies absolutely. Whilst his playing was modernized, at the same time he accomplished, in my opinion, the revival of the tradition of the eighteenth-century virtuoso. He carries on the tradition from the very fact of his choice of an instrument which had been thoroughly despised, and of his raising it to the highest level of technical and artistic achievement. The harsh, primitive double-bass, extricated by him from the depths of the orchestra, he transformed into an instrument of the most delicate musical expression, and an object of splendour.

In Berlin Koussevitzky became acquainted with all the leading composers and artists. One might meet in his hospitable home all the members of Berlin's select artistic circle.

Towards the end of his residence his activities as a conductor underwent considerable development. His transition from instrumental or orchestral virtuosity became an accomplished fact. He definitely decided that in this was the fundamental meaning of his vocation, and he gave himself up entirely to it. From occupying the lowliest place in the orchestra as a double-bass player, he was now promoted to the highest — the conductor's desk. Before him were revealed new prospects, new aims and aspirations.

The preliminary technical and educational training in the art of conducting having been completed in Berlin, the second and most important period of his activity began. In this connexion he had to decide whether to stay in Europe and establish his position in the international musical arena or to return to Russia and link up his work with the general process of the musical life of that country in the state of development which it had then reached. He was inclined to remain in Europe, but came to the conclusion that it was more necessary and fruitful to work for his native land. He determined to transfer the centre of gravity and the basis of all his activities to Russia.

About this time Koussevitzky conceived the idea of starting a venture of his own for the publication of music. It was his intention on his return to Russia to extend his activities beyond those usually associated with an orchestral conductor and to take part in the general musical life of the country.

The organization of a publishing firm on entirely new lines, such aş had not been attempted in the past, was one of the first problems which confronted him. It was a time of idealism and romantic visions, which came into being simultaneously with the new century. The art of Europe and Russia was reanimated by fresh and reviving breezes. Daring and unusual projects were devised; all the young men were full of audacity and searching new ways. Koussevitzky's scheme for the organization of a new and special type of music-publishing business was idealistic in its conception, but was put by him on a sound and practical footing.

The most brilliant and prominent name in Russian music at that time was Aleksandr Nikolaevich Scriabin. He was in the fullest sense the master of the minds of the younger Russian generation, and the idol of all who were in the front line of Russian culture.

In 1908 Koussevitzky paid a visit to Scriabin,

who was then living in Lausanne, working in solitude at his plans and at the realization of his most important works. These years in Switzerland were the time of his final ripening and his attainment of spiritual maturity; after them came the concluding period of his life in Russia — the period of the supreme expansion and revelation of his creative powers.

Koussevitzky went to Lausanne in order to offer Scriabin an interest in the projected publishing business and was successful in his mission.

Thus was laid the foundation of an acquaintance which had such an enormous significance in the lives and activities of the two musicians.

In 1909 the Koussevitzkys arrived in Moscow. . . .

CHAPTER SIX

*Berlin at the Beginning of the
Twentieth Century*

IN THOSE DAYS BERLIN WAS BEYOND QUESTION THE official centre of the music, not only of Europe, but of the world. It was the focus of the world's musical culture, attracting to itself all that was best and most valuable at the time. It was the source from which the musical streams flowed in all directions. It is true that there were also two other centres, but their spheres of influence were far more restricted than Berlin's. In relation to world-music they might be regarded as provincial centres: Paris, for young Latin Europe; and St. Petersburg and Moscow, for eastern Europe. At that time everything that was created in Paris was manifestly opposed to and aimed directly at Germany. Musical impressionism started in Paris, as a revolt against the hegemony of the German musical culture, against its musical scholasticism, its classicism, and above all against the post-romantic heritage left by Wagner. The main ideas of French impressionism were not of a musical order, but were derived from and nourished by French impressionist painting. In this we have simultaneously the strength and the weakness of the movement.

In Russia there was no opposition to Berlin. The official Russian musical culture of the time voluntarily and without question recognized itself to be a province under the sway of the German musical centre, with which it considered itself organically connected. Hardly a voice of protest or independence was raised against this subjection. If any such were occasionally heard, it was too feeble and isolated to constitute any serious danger to the existing state of things.

Thus, officially, Berlin was the centre of the musical "empire."

The official bases of Berlin musical culture were represented in those days by a series of events of first-rate artistic importance. To begin with, there were the Philharmonic orchestral concerts under the direction of Nikisch, which for that period were the supreme examples of the technique of conducting and the mastery of symphonic interpretation. Here was the fundamental basis of the conductor's art, created from the elements of individualistic romanticism, semi-improvisational pathos, and the intuitive method. Nikisch's intuitive method combined entire freedom of interpretation and a regard for the tradition normalizing that freedom. He always subjected the caprice and waywardness of his artistic temperament to the inner logic of the works he was performing, thereby creating an æsthetic equilibrium and unity of form and content. Amongst conductors Nikisch was the favourite and recognized leader of romanticism and the post-romantic school.

Koussevitzky was trained in accordance with the principles established by Nikisch. If his interpretations are to be connected with any of the great traditions of the early twentieth century, it must be with Nikisch, with whom he has far more in common than with the other conductors of that period.

Side by side with Nikisch's concerts were those given by the orchestra of the Berlin Opera under Felix Weingartner. This was a sort of free academy, devoted mainly to the cultivation of Beethoven. Weingartner specialized in the interpretation of Beethoven's symphonic works, both in the concert room and in his theoretical writings, and acquired universal fame in this connexion. His authority on the subject was so firmly established that any other performer of Beethoven's music had seriously to reckon with it.

Besides the concerts of Nikisch and Weingartner, there were incidental concerts under the direction of such great masters of the orchestra as Felix Mottl, Schuch, and Gustav Mahler. The last-named played an entirely independent role.

Though perhaps the most notable conductor of his day, officially Mahler was by no means so generally accepted and appreciated as Nikisch. Mahler explored the profundities of the music and was therefore beyond the depth of many of his hearers, whereas Nikisch was comprehensible to the average man.

If we recall the monumental choral concerts, the performances under Siegfried Ochs at the Opera, with its premières of works which created a sensation, such as Richard Strauss's *Salome, Elektra,* and *Der Rosenkavalier,* conducted by the composer, and Tchaikovsky's *The Queen of Spades,* under Leo Blech, and the concert appearances of famous stars from all parts of the world — it seems to me that we shall have given an idea of the official chronicle of Berlin as the musical centre of the world at the beginning of the twentieth century.

In the creative sphere Richard Strauss undoubtedly occupied the first place. His modernism in its general features found expression in the development of the principles of Liszt's and Berlioz's program music, on the basis of the prevailing æstheticophilosophical, individualistic tendencies, which Strauss transformed into musical productions. They presented a combination, strange in those days, but very powerful and convincing, of naturalism and fantasticism.

The other wing of modernism, which sought to connect itself with the purely German traditions, found an advocate in the person of the fertile, semi-romantic, semi-scholastic Max Reger, in whom Russia was also greatly interested. In academic circles, there was the cult of Brahms. Probably it was just because these people considered Brahms to be their exclusive and inalienable property, contrasting his music with everything new and vital that was being produced at the time — probably it was for this very reason that the younger generation of musicians experienced an unconquerable aversion to him, which endured for nearly the whole of the first quarter of the twentieth century and from which it is now difficult to recover. Even today musicians are divisible into two categories — those who " still " love Brahms and those who " already " love him, which is by no means one and the same thing. . . .

This period also witnessed the awakening of a serious interest in Bruckner, whose pure and austere music Berlin had hitherto been unable to understand.

On the ultra-modernist flank the voice of Arnold Schönberg — anarchical intellectualist and extreme individualist — began to make itself more and more loudly heard from the musical "cellar." In after years he was destined, under the influence of the war and the revolution, to dominate for a certain time the ideas of the new generation of German musicians and even to originate a special movement in music — so-called atonal music.

In the course of these years the development of Berlin's musical life reached its culminating point. After this it began to decline, mainly owing to the expansion of French musical impressionism on the one hand and to the "anarchy" brought about by Schönberg on the other. French impressionism dealt a blow from without at the supports of German musical culture, which had seemed to be almost proof against shock; whilst the atonal anarchy, for which Schönberg was responsible, loosened them from within.

Having demolished the foundations of German music in the form in which they existed at the beginning of the new century (that is, a combination of the heritage of classicism and the product of the later romanticism, which exactly represent the early characteristics of the modernist style), French impressionism, created by Debussy, and atonal expressionism, created by Schönberg, starting from opposite national and cultural premises, came into collision with each other on the body of German music. The ultimate result of this collision was the reaction of one upon the other, which took place on the collapse of the German national musical culture. The revival of that culture did not begin until after the failure of Germany's military power and was accomplished in a new era and under other conditions.

PART II

CHAPTER SEVEN

A Glance at History

THE MOST TRYING CIRCUMSTANCE FOR THE MAJOR-
ity of those who came into the world in the latter part
of the nineteenth century is the cleavage which takes
place in their consciousness and their sentiments on
the border line separating it from the twentieth century. They were born in the one that is past, but all
their experiences belong to the other. Their roots are
in the nineteenth century, their fruit-bearing branches
were put forth in the twentieth.

Koussevitzky belongs to the category of contemporary artists who bear within themselves this dualism of two cultures. On the one hand he is under the sway of the heritage of the past century, on which he was brought up and with which he is organically connected; on the other he has witnessed and participated in the collapse of that culture and the creation of its successor. In these two processes the meaning of all that characterizes the men of that time is comprised. I do not know if the birth of any previous century has been attended with so much suffering or has been so prolonged and difficult.

Koussevitzky was also one of those who excavated the tunnel which provided an outlet from the nineteenth to the twentieth century. The first two decades of the latter were heroic years for him, the central period of his life, since they were particularly connected with memories of the collapse and death of the old and the coming of the new. The bitter and obstinate struggle between the century that had departed into eternity and its successor continued for twenty years. The new arrival had not yet revealed its true features and still retained its mysterious mask, as it

KAZAN by ROBERT STERL

were, but it persistently asserted its rights and cleared the way for the future.

It was a veritable duel to the death.

With the war and the revolution we Russians finally broke through into the twentieth century, after which a return to the past proved to be entirely out of the question. The winter of 1913–14 was the last banquet given by the nineteenth century in honour of its descendants. Essentially, however, it was feasting while the plague was rampant; it was almost a funeral festivity.[1]

The revolutionary explosion of 1918 hurled us definitely and with terrible force into the twentieth century, into a world with new standards of measurement, into a new order of things. The history of the culture of these two decades is nothing more than the history of the contest between the old and the new styles. It is the history of the relations which formerly existed between man and the world and of those which replaced them.

What sort of role does music play in this process?

---

[1] *Trizna.* An ancient heathen function in memory of the dead. It comprised a banquet, public games, and races. TRANSLATOR.

It is very difficult and rather awkward to speak of it
" professionally." You see, this historical process in
its entirety was " music." It was the agitated element,
dark and turbid, which cast up on the shores of life
that which was hidden in the abyss of its chaos let
loose.

Only when included by us in our cosmic order,
in the pitiful everyday life of contemporary man,
were these gifts, the product of the element of the historical process, classified in accordance with the sym-
bols of professionalism and of the particular form of
cultural activity to which they belonged — to the
savant, the constructor, the politician.

If we bestow a cursory glance on the state of
music in Russia at the beginning of the twentieth century, we shall see that it presents a very complex and
tangled combination of mutual relations. Generaliz-
ing these relations and reducing them by the method
of simplification to a common denominator, we come
up against two fundamental tendencies differing from
and hostile to each other. They prove to be in conformity with the general cultural and historical process of Russia and find their reflection in music accord-

ing as they have been characteristic of the state of Russian thought — philosophic, æsthetic, or generally political and social. These tendencies in the Russian music of that period have their counterparts in what were known as Westernism and Slavophilism in the general process of Russian culture and history. Though in the other branches of Russian culture these tendencies, whilst still existing, had been very much toned down and smoothed over at the beginning of the twentieth century, and manifested themselves through the prism of very complex mental temperaments (already of quite a new and different order), in Russian music, which was rather in arrear of the general cultural and historical process — as music always and everywhere is — the collision between Westernism and Slavophilism, tendencies inherited directly from the ideology of the end of the nineteenth century, was clearly audible to the attentive ear and occupied a position in the foreground of Russian musical life.

The nationalists, than whom none were sincerer in their ideas, held that Russian culture in general and Russian music in particular should be absolutely independent of western Europe. Their adherents were

the development of Russian music at the end of the nineteenth and the beginning of the twentieth centuries was expressed in vacillation, in the choice between this or the other line of action — that is, between a rapprochement with the culture of western Europe, on the one hand, and a development to the utmost of the specifically Russian national element, on the other. Essentially this amounts to nothing else than a choice between the attractions of this element (since the whole essence of Russian national music, its specific quality, consists in fusion with it) and the seductions of culture, involving subjection to the formal and æsthetic canon which is the basic, organizing principle of western European music. Russian musicians have long since devoted their matured efforts to the latter, have striven to overcome the " provincialism " of Russian music and the exoticism which is particularly characteristic of it. They have desired to stand on a level with the general development of western European music, not in the position of a junior who is repeating experiments which western Europe has already made, but on an equal footing.

In connexion with this the whole of Russian

music since Glinka falls into two halves, as it were, bisected by these two fundamental tendencies which have always existed in it. They found their supreme creative expression in the music of Moussorgsky, the most powerful exponent of the purely national problem in music, on the one hand, and in the works of Tchaikovsky, who was the most pronounced "Westerner," on the other. From a historical point of view, all the rest are grouped round these two musicians, in accordance with the tendencies I have indicated.

This schematic presentation is, of course, very primitive and conditional and applies only in so far as it is a question of the ideological trend of Russian music. That is why Tchaikovsky, in spite of his love for and subjection to the canon of western Europe, is not less of a Russian musician than Moussorgsky, as many people in Europe mistakenly suppose him to be. Similarly it is impossible to share the monstrously crude and mistaken opinion, held by many Russian "Westerners" to this day, that Moussorgsky's music is a formless, half-educated barbarism.

Debussy, who in the twentieth century gave us in new music a most delicate and subtle exposition of

ASTRAKHAN by ROBERT STERL

style, form, and canon, was brought up on Moussorgsky, was nourished by him; in his time, therefore, he provided in his creative work a most convincing defence of Moussorgsky's significance and grasp of form.

A special place in Russian music is occupied by Rimsky-Korsakov, who, at the time of its greatest expansion, tried to restore the synthesis created by Glinka and lost after his death. But the fact is, as I have already stated, Glinka's synthesis was limited. In it was the living, creatively attained combination of the elementary processes of folk-music and the organizing formal canon. Rimsky-Korsakov did not succeed. His synthesis was of a mechanical, and not an organic, nature. To the same extent his feeling for and comprehension of the folk-element (the national pathos) was not a living force, but a conventional quantity, as conventional as the whole of the formal structure of his works. Possessing an extensive professional musical experience, which gave him great authority, Rimsky-Korsakov's whole life was devoted to restoring order in the Russian musical household. He combed it and tidied it, applying Beckmesser's rule to everything created by Russian musicians, including, of course, all his own things. He set out his calculations on Beckmesser's slate, which by a curious whim of destiny became the heritage of this musician, who, by a mistake of Nature, was born in Russia and not in Germany, to which he looked all his life, seeking justification, approval, and support for himself in a pseudo-classical German academicism and in the " infallible truths " of its scholasticism. . . .

I have paused to glance at the fundamental tendencies of Russian music because they were in full accord with the general condition and development of Russian musical life at this period and gave the keynote to all the rest. Mention of them is necessary to an understanding of the process of Russian musical culture, which otherwise would be quite incomprehensible.

CHAPTER EIGHT

The Publishing Venture

KOUSSEVITZKY RETURNED TO RUSSIA IN 1909 AND
settled down in Moscow, where he immediately made
himself talked about. He became one of the most
striking figures on the horizon of Moscow's musical
life. He was the centre of brawls and seething pas-
sions. When he left Moscow in 1905, it was to travel
abroad as a star performer on the double-bass; as
such everybody knew him, and it was only as such
that he had obtained recognition in his native land,

in Russia. It is true that they regarded him as a quite exceptional soloist on the double-bass, but beyond that they knew nothing of him. On his return in 1909 he at once demanded to be treated from an entirely different standpoint. His activities as a double-bass soloist were relegated to a secondary place, and he put in a very serious claim to his rights on the concert platform as an orchestral conductor and to a share in the general musical life of Moscow. At the same time his independent financial position gave him a free hand in the matter of the schemes for his new undertakings, which he proceeded to put into operation in a very independent fashion, regardless of anybody or anything except the purposes he had in mind. In musical, social, and official circles a definitely hostile attitude towards him was immediately assumed. He became a serious rival of the leading spirits in the musical life of Moscow, and from their point of view introduced " disorders " disturbing and entangling the " politics " of the day. The ill will displayed towards him was so openly and implacably hostile that he would have been completely paralysed and would have been able to accomplish absolutely none of his intentions but for his exceptional musical gifts, his material independence, and his energy, which served him as his best defence, thrusting him to the front and vanquishing the adverse forces.

Koussevitzky came forth in the role of an advanced " Westerner." He appeared in Moscow as a cultured European and began to set on foot a series of enterprises entirely new in those days. In the course of his first year in Moscow he organized his own publishing firm, under the name of " The Russian Music-Publishing House." Its aims were idealistic and not commercial; it laid itself out to publish new, important, and bulky works which had met with no support from other publishers, but its main object was the propaganda of modern Russian music. A more vigorous development of the latter in Russia had begun, and it was taking the place of the musical movement associated with the Belaev establishment, which had been founded by the Russian Mæcenas with the sole object of propagating Russian music and encouraging and helping young Russian composers. At that time, however, owing to insufficiency of funds and the lack of a successor to carry on the Belaev

artistic tradition after the founder's death, it had begun to languish; it published a steadily decreasing
number of new works and depended for its existence
mainly on the reissue of publications brought out in
Belaev's lifetime. Young composers found it increasingly difficult to be published by Belaev, unless they
followed the beaten track or had some official musical
backing. Thus, shortly after Belaev's death the business founded by him in support of an ideal lost its
vital significance and was gradually transformed into
an ordinary commercial undertaking, in which form
it dragged out a rather sorry existence, with very
limited resources.

Belaev was impelled to become a publisher by
his desire to give young Glazounov's compositions to
the world. The business grew and brought within its
scope the activities of the "mighty band "[1] and the
musicians who adhered to it and were connected with
it, excepting only Moussorgsky, whom Bessel had
"devoured."

The work accomplished by Belaev's publishing

---

[1] Balakirev, Borodin, Cui, Moussorgsky, and Rimsky-Korsakov,
who founded what is known as the "Russian National School."
TRANSLATOR.

house was of great value and importance at that time. He published the compositions of the " mighty band " and spread them far and wide, in western Europe as well as in Russia, by means of the press and by organizing periodically the concerts known as the " Russian Symphony Concerts."

Belaev's activities, which had begun with young Glazounov, ended with young Scriabin, the first half of whose creative work came into his hands. This was no small matter, but when Belaev died and the business deteriorated, Scriabin had no more to do with it. He had already, in his younger days, met with determined opposition on the part of the musicians who were the leading spirits in Belaev's undertaking and the authoritative exponents of its aims. Scriabin had entirely dropped out of the orbit of their outlook on the world and their artistic ideals. When he was younger, he was retained in the Belaev business solely by the personal and powerful support of the publisher himself, whose exceptional sense of values kept him abreast of the times. In 1909 Scriabin was without a publisher, as the Belaev undertaking declined to accept his compositions on account of lack of means and reduced his honorarium by one half. He then became his own publisher and printed the Fifth Sonata, but did not know how to put it on the market. When Koussevitzky visited Scriabin at Lausanne, he saw stacks of this sonata lying about, the composer being quite at a loss to know what to do with them.

Koussevitzky's publishing practically took the place of Belaev's, just as modernism supplanted the tendencies connected with the activities of the " mighty band."

The Russian Music-Publishing House opened up new prospects especially for the younger Russian composers and met with a very sympathetic reception.

Sergei Taneiev was delighted to hear of the new enterprise and to receive an invitation to participate in it.

" Now I shall realize my dream of long ago," he said, "to write a big cantata on the text of Khomyakov's *On Reading a Psalm*. I've never been able to do it till now, because nobody would have published it. Besides, I couldn't spare the time for it, as I was busy with small things and with lessons, by which I earned my living."

Taneiev received an honorarium in advance and devoted the whole of his time to this cantata. It was finished in 1914 and was performed by Koussevitzky in Moscow and St. Petersburg during the season of 1914–15. It gave the composer great delight and was the last work which he was to enjoy, as he died in 1915.

The other publishing firms carrying on business in Russia at the time were the ordinary undertakings, pursuing purely commercial ends and exploiting the composers. They refused to bring out any big works and confined themselves almost entirely to songs and piano pieces. As a result of this state of things composers ceased to write in the larger forms. The classical instance of this exploitation was Moussorgsky's, of whose fate everybody was aware. Bessel gave him hardly anything for his compositions and literally nothing at all for many of them and retained the " perpetual " copyright. On the death of Moussorgsky, Bessel proved to be the sole proprietor of nearly all his music and he exploited his " rights " as miraculously as the owners of mineral wealth, guarding them jealously until quite recently, when, in accordance with the law protecting authors' rights, they were taken from him. His ill-omened treatment of Moussorgsky is unparalleled in the history of music and far surpasses anything else we know of the obdurate exploitation of composers at any time or in any place.

The Russian Music-Publishing House arrived like an oasis in the desert of the other establishments. It refused on principle to exploit the composers, and set up as its aim the publication of any music of sufficient merit, regardless of its dimensions, nor did it matter whether it was the work of a famous composer or of a young beginner.

The honorarium paid by it was very liberal for those days. In addition, the composer received royalties of twenty-five per cent up to the moment when the cost of publication was covered, and then it was doubled. The Russian Music-Publishing House was founded for Russian composers only. Its articles were drawn up by S. A. Muromtsev, president of the first State Duma. The original capital was one million roubles.

In view of the fact that Russian publishers did not sign the Berne Convention, and the works of

Russian composers were therefore not safeguarded against the possibility of reprints, Koussevitzky's business was registered in Germany.

When a series of compositions had been issued, music shops were opened in Moscow and St. Petersburg. They were run on western European lines, stocking foreign editions, all the new musical publications, and rare examples of old music.

At first things went smoothly, but in a short time friction arose. There was no trouble on the business and technical side. The composers were much interested, the edition was tasteful in appearance and attractive to the eye — Koussevitzky commissioned Bilibin, the artist, to design the cover. The unpleasantness began from within, amongst the small committee or jury whose duty it was to select new musical works for publication. Koussevitzky did not wish to take sole personal charge of the business, since in founding it with an ideal and not a commercial aim in view he had imparted to it a character almost resembling that of an art society. Lest it should be at the mercy of individual carprice in matters of taste, Koussevitzky organized an art jury in connexion with the business, who were to decide as to the acceptance or rejection of new works. This jury consisted of Rachmaninoff, Scriabin, Medtner, Ossovsky, Koussevitzky, and Struve (business manager). Some of the members, not realizing what the new business stood for, took up a manifestly hostile position in regard to manuscripts suggested for publication which bore the impress of originality, freshness, and novelty. The more original a composition, the greater was the hostility, sometimes implacable, displayed by these gentlemen. As often happens in organizations of this kind — musical or artistic — men invited as helpers became hindrances, revealing themselves as a reactionary force which threatened to mutilate the meaning of all that Koussevitzky had devised. Scriabin of course was the exception. Entirely absorbed in his own creative work, in which he burned as in a consuming fire, Scriabin's attitude towards the art of others was one of utter indifference and impassiveness, but to anything new he was invariably sympathetic and benevolent.

When Koussevitzky saw how the jury were treating a matter that was very dear to him, he grew irritable. The relations between him and certain of the members were seriously strained, and once, when Stravinsky's *Petrushka* was rejected on the pretext that it was "not music," he announced that he would withdraw from the jury unless they altered their mind. This was the only argument that convinced them of the advisability of accepting *Petrushka* for publication. Prokofiev's *Scythian Suite* was also declined by some members of the jury, but in this instance Koussevitzky did not fall back on threats. He sought another way out of the difficulty — by buying Gutheil's publishing business, for which he paid 250,-000 roubles. He turned it into a branch of the Russian Music-Publishing House, and there he accepted works which pleased him, without consulting any kind of jury.

CHAPTER NINE

Concerts
(St. Petersburg, Moscow, and the Volga Tour)

KOUSSEVITZKY ANNOUNCED HIS FIRST CYCLE OF symphony concerts during the Moscow season of 1909–10. Known as the "Sergei Koussevitzky Symphonic Concerts," they became exceptionally popular with the public and the younger generation.

For this first season he called in the services of the orchestra of the Imperial Theatres. The concerts were given in the hall at the "Noblemen's Assembly." At that time there were no concert agents in

Russia, and Koussevitzky and his wife had to attend to all the arrangements. They divided the work, Natalya Konstantinovna undertaking the technical and administrative side, whilst Sergei Alexandrovich confined himself to the purely artistic details.

In spite of the manifest ill will of the official musical organizations and the press, if not all at once, at all events within the first year these concerts ranked amongst the most important artistic events of the Moscow season.

Side by side with the Moscow concerts Koussevitzky gave another series in St. Petersburg, where they were carried on under the flag of the Russian Musical Society. The Concerts of the Russian Musical Society had been instituted by Anton Rubinstein, but had gradually fallen into decay and degenerated into a feeble organization, which performed its duties in a spirit of routine. Essentially it had existed under the Conservatory, which was also subject to the jurisdiction of the Russian Musical Society. At that time the concerts were carried on with the help of the students' orchestra and the co-operation of the Conservatory professors. Really, then, they were Conservatory concerts, formerly confined to the school, but subsequently made available to the general public. The latter attended them very reluctantly, in view of the musty odour which clung to them, the dull, uninteresting programs, and the second-rate soloists. The blame for all this must, of course, be ascribed to the usual deterioration, routinism, and want of culture of the leaders and above all to the absence of the spirit of a real, living art. Naturally these concerts always had a deficit, and hence the Russian Musical Society, delighted at the possibility of getting them off its hands, if only for once, proposed that Koussevitzky should take upon himself the organization of the concerts for one season, subject to the proviso that he cover the deficit. To this he agreed.

The appearance of Sergei Koussevitzky's name on the Russian Musical Society's bills was a surprise. It was like a breath of fresh air to see something new and unusual in connexion with these concerts. The innovations introduced by Koussevitzky, by the way, included analytical programs of the works to be played.

PROGRAM OF A KOUSSEVITZKY
CONCERT IN MOSCOW AND
PETROGRAD—1909
(*Drawn by Dobujinsky*)

In the following season (1910–11) he formed a
symphonic orchestra of his own, consisting of eighty-
five musicians chosen by competitive examination.
They were engaged for the year and were not allowed
to play anywhere else.

For three months before the concerts Koussevitzky worked at Beethoven's symphonies with this
orchestra. It was the preliminary training which it
underwent preparatory to its first appearance with
him before the public.

Koussevitzky's own orchestra cost him a hundred thousand roubles a year. During the same season he organized in Moscow a chorus of two hundred
and fifty voices, and in St. Petersburg he invited
Arkhangelsky's choir to assist him.

Arkhangelsky's name should be remembered
with gratitude for the immense and exceedingly valuable work he accomplished in implanting the cult of
choral music in Russia.

With the formation of an orchestra of his own
the Sergei Koussevitzky concerts acquired a solid and
independent footing. Henceforth they no longer came
into contact with other official concert organizations,

but carried on their work quite independently. Every season a cycle of symphony concerts was given, once a week regularly, on Wednesdays, in Moscow and St. Petersburg, performing the same program in both cities, with the assistance of the same soloists. They travelled from St. Petersburg to Moscow by special train. The concerts began in the middle of October and went on until the middle of February, till the beginning of Lent. It was obligatory in Russia to suspend all state and private theatrical performances and all concerts and entertainments of any sort during Lent. This custom is explained by the fact that the State safeguarded the religious cult established by the Church.

Koussevitzky was the first to introduce students' tickets at a very low price (fifty copecks), thus enabling the younger generation to hear serious music. These tickets became exceptionally popular; and as the number was limited, the young people stood in queues in order to get them.

In the spring of 1911 Koussevitzky gave a grand cycle of Beethoven concerts (the first in Russia) in Moscow and St. Petersburg. After the summer in-

terval, during which there were concerts at Sokolniki, near Moscow, he toured the southern provinces of Russia — this was in the autumn of 1911.
He visited Kiev, Kharkov, Odessa, and Rostov-on-
Don, and at every place he performed a complete
cycle of Beethoven's works. On each of these
tours his appearances were attended with unusual success and the enthusiastic gratitude of the
rising generation, for whom the concerts were a real
treat.

Simultaneously with the symphony concerts
Koussevitzky instituted Sunday concerts, the programs
consisting of compositions within the reach of the
general public. In a way they were popular concerts,
open to everyone, at a charge of ten copecks for admission. He did not conduct them himself, but put his
orchestra at the disposal of young conductors, thus
giving them an opportunity of testing their powers
and gaining experience. Budding soloists were also
allowed to take part in these concerts, and amongst
those who made their first public appearances on
this platform were the pianists Orlov, Borovsky, and
others.

Koussevitzky also arranged a series of chamber concerts, which were carried on side by side with the others.

In the autumn of 1912 he organized a Tchaikovsky festival in Moscow. The composer's brother, Modest Tchaikovsky, who was present at all the concerts, remarked: "So long as Koussevitzky performs my brother's compositions, the music of Tchaikovsky will live." These words were in the nature of a reply to the attacks on Tchaikovsky's art which were current at that time.

A Bach festival in both capitals in the spring of 1913 was followed by a provincial tour in the autumn, with Tchaikovsky programs.

Every season Koussevitzky shared his concerts with star conductors, whom he invited from Europe, and with composers, who conducted their own works on such occasions.

Arthur Nikisch, who was a close friend of his, was a visiting conductor every year from the inception of the orchestra.

Koussevitzky speaks with great feeling of Debussy's visit to Russia, whither he came on Kousse-

vitzky's invitation to conduct his own compositions in
St. Petersburg and Moscow. The programs included
*La Mer, Nocturnes, L'Après-midi d'un faune, Ronde
de printemps, Iberia, Gigues,* the Rhapsodie for clarinet and orchestra, etc.

During Debussy's three weeks in Russia he
stayed with the Koussevitzkys. His hours of leisure he
spent at the piano. Disliking publicity, he never appeared at concerts as a soloist, but confined his playing to a small circle of his intimate friends. Debussy's
scores are preserved at Koussevitzky's house, with
the composer's annotations — tokens of their joint
labours and friendly discussions.

Debussy had not been in Russia since his twentieth year, when he had come at the invitation of N. von
Meck. On this second visit he went to see von Meck's
house, then owned by the father of Madame Koussevitzky, which had precious memories for him. Here
he had first made the acquaintance of Moussorgsky's
compositions. Tchaikovsky's creative work was also
closely connected with the von Meck family, who were
eminent patrons of music.

Debussy had an exceptionally warm reception

in Russia. In modernist circles banquets and gatherings were arranged in his honour.

The finest soloists of the day appeared by invitation on Koussevitzky's platform. Among them were:

> Pianists: Rachmaninoff, Scriabin, Busoni, Sauer, Godowsky, Schnabel, Medtner, Bauer, Risler, and others
>
> Singers: Julia Culp, Felia Litvine, Elena Gerhardt
>
> Violinists: Kreisler, Auer, Heifetz, Marteau, Elman.

To assist in the big ensembles he called in the leading soloists of the Imperial Theatres: Nezhdanova, Zbrueva, Alchevsky, Sobinov, Ershov. Ludwig Wüllner came for the *Manfred* performance.

The Director of the Imperial Theatres, Telyakovsky, appreciating the cultural side of Koussevitzky's concerts, always went out of his way to oblige him and sometimes changed the repertory of the theatre in order that his soloists might be able to appear on Koussevitzky's platform. Telyakovsky was an exception amongst Imperial Theatre directors. He

SERGEI KOUSSEVITZKY at a concert during the Volga Tour in 1912, by
ROBERT STERL

was a cultured man, but some of his predecessors, officials appointed by the Government to look after the Theatres, knew absolutely nothing about art.

A comical story is told of one such director, a general, who, on inspecting the orchestra, inquired: " Who are these people? "

" First violins," was the reply.

" And these? "

" Second violins."

The general was indignant. " What! " he roared. " Second violins in an Imperial Theatre! . . . Clear them out! "

Amongst Russian concert associations Koussevitzky's unquestionably held the most important place in Moscow. His concerts were distinguished by the advanced nature of the programs and the very high standard of performance. They were attended by connoisseurs and representatives of the most cultured section of Moscow society.

In St. Petersburg these concerts ranked on a par with A. Siloti's; he had entered the field before Koussevitzky and like him took a line of his own and held advanced views on music.

At this period the Russian capitals relied for their concerts on the following organizations: the Russian Musical Society, which was connected with the St. Petersburg and Moscow conservatories; the Russian Symphony Concerts, run in conjunction with Belaev's publishing business; and the Siloti and Koussevitzky concerts. Siloti's orchestra did not play in Moscow, but that city had the Philharmonic Society's concerts, whose programs displayed the same tendencies as those of the Russian Musical Society.

Just as the Belaev and the Russian Musical Society's concerts assumed an increasingly conservative character and receded into the background, so Koussevitzky and Siloti in St. Petersburg endeavoured to perform all that was best in the sphere of creative music at the time, attracting to themselves the greatest forces in the musical world, the most distinguished Russian and European artists. Debussy appeared with Koussevitzky; Siloti first introduced Schönberg to Russia, by giving a concert at which the latter conducted a program of his own compositions.

Rivalry of this kind greatly stimulated the musical life of St. Petersburg, and the artistic importance of the concerts increased with every season. They were beyond question significant events, and a joy to all young people who were ardently devoted to the cause of art.

To complete the portrait of the musical life of Russia at that period I append an excerpt from the memoirs of my friend the poet Mandelstamm. His vivid and picturesque description in which he re-creates the atmosphere surrounding the Koussevitzky concerts in Moscow and St. Petersburg could not be bettered. "Here was no musical dilettantism," he writes, "but something threatening, even deadly, arose from the depths, something resembling a long-ing for action, an obscure prehistoric restlessness. In the hazy light of the gas-lamps the lordly edifice with many porticos was regularly besieged. The prancing mounted gendarmes, imparting to the atmosphere of the square a suggestion of civil disorder, clattered about and shouted, guarding the main entrance. Through the triple ranks carriages with springs and dim lamps crept in and arranged themselves in an imposing black camp. The cabmen did not venture to drive up to the building itself — they had been paid their fares on the way — and they slipped out, avoiding the wrath of the police. The St. Petersburger like a feverish little fish entered the marble ice-hole of the vestibule, disappearing into the glowing house of ice, rigged out with silk and velvet. The stalls and the seats behind them were crowded as usual, but the vast galleries off the side entrances were packed, and looked like baskets filled with clusters of human grapes. In the galleries a July temperature. In the air a perpetual shrilling, like the cicadas on the steppe."

The Koussevitzky concerts were the concerts of a free symphonic association. In its organization and its aims it was subject only to the will of its permanent director, Sergei Koussevitzky himself, who was the sole and omnipotent proprietor of the undertaking.

Under such conditions it was of course possible to do something, and not a little was achieved.

First of all, the Koussevitzky concerts became a carefully planned nursery of serious symphonic music in Russia; they were analogous to the great symphonic associations of Berlin, Vienna, London, and Paris.

Thanks to them the classical foundations of symphonic music were durably implanted in the consciousness of Russian audiences. The great festivals of the works of Bach, Beethoven, and Brahms educated the public in the severer examples of musical creation. Koussevitzky's visits with his orchestra to the provincial towns of Russia helped to instil a knowledge of serious music in the minds of a wide circle of the population, many of whom had never heard a single serious musical work nor suspected the existence of performances of such a high standard and had not even known what a big symphony orchestra was like. Koussevitzky's Volga tours played an important part in the popularizing of music amongst the inhabitants of an extensive area.

In the spring of 1910, at the close of the St. Petersburg and Moscow concert season, Koussevitzky took his full orchestra, assisted by specially invited soloists, down the Volga. The tour was repeated in 1912 and 1914. On each occasion they gave concerts at all the big towns on both banks of the river: Tver, Rybinsk, Yaroslavl, Kostroma, Nizhny Novgorod, Kazan, Simbirsk, Samara, Saratov, Tsaritsyn,

Astrakhan. The concerts began at Tver and ended at
Astrakhan. A passenger steamer was chartered and
was at Koussevitzky's disposal for the full length of
the tour — five or six weeks.

Scriabin, by the way, was one of the soloists on
the first occasion, and Risler on the third. In addition to the performers the company included Koussevitzky's friends and guests — a number of artists and
art workers — whom he had invited from Europe.

Several years later, during the war, Professor
Sterl, Director of the Dresden Academy, and Oscar
Bie, the well-known German writer and art critic,
collaborated on a volume of recollections of their
voyage down the Volga with Koussevitzky, which had
impressed itself indelibly on their memories.

To appreciate the romantic charm of these voy-
ages — in which the impressions of the marvels of
nature were succeeded by feasts of music, amidst the
wonderful architecture of the ancient Volga towns —
one must know what the Volga is and what it is like in
spring, when it begins to rise.

The concert time-table was rigidly adhered to,
but apart from that they travelled at their leisure,

stopping where they felt inclined, organizing picnics, and visiting places of interest. Thus, for instance, on one of the tours they inspected the nomad villages of the Buddhist Kalmucks, who had their own temple on the Volga. They also visited the fisheries near Astrakhan and the villages of the German colonists, which had been in existence since the time of Catherine.

At Tsaritsyn Koussevitzky gave a concert for the workers, which made such a powerful impression that on his next visit he found they had started an amateur orchestra, dedicated to the name of Koussevitzky. His concerts on the Volga created something in the nature of a sensation amongst the inhabitants, who had never heard anything like it. At one town where a concert was announced, a delegation from the leading merchants waited on Koussevitzky to request that the harp should be given a very prominent place on the platform, in order that they might see what the instrument was like and how it was played.

The " wandering " musicians were to these places the bringers of culture, fantasy, and myth. . . .

CHAPTER TEN

The Modernists

KOUSSEVITZKY ALLOTTED A CONSIDERABLE SHARE OF his programs to the new musical works which were then making their appearance in western Europe and which he wished to introduce to the Russian public. At this period the French impressionists were at the height of their powers, and Koussevitzky, who followed with a lively interest everything new in art, became a zealous performer of Debussy, Ravel, and other composers belonging to the movement. Debussy, the creator and most eminent exponent of musical impressionism, obtained in Koussevitzky an ideal interpreter of his orchestral works. From the very beginning Koussevitzky's readings of Debussy were distinguished by unusual refinement, thoughtfulness, and spirituality. Contact between him and Debussy was naturally and immediately established. The world of that fragile and exquisite musical painting, bathed in a slightly intoxicating and bewildering atmosphere, found a ready response in Koussevitzky's sensitive musical and æsthetic tastes and temperament. It is rarely that composer and performer are so closely drawn to each other. And, most important of all, Debussy found in Koussevitzky a conductor whose technique was organically suited to his principles of composition. This is worthy of note, since these are fundamental and not casual questions.

The most characteristic feature in Debussy's music is that in it rhythm, and not metre, plays a predominant part. His metres are nearly always of a rhapsodical nature, by virtue of which they are based, not on a measured movement, but on an almost constant rubato.

It is only at the starting-points in various parts of a composition that Debussy's metre acquires its normal meaning of measured movement. Metre serves to set him going at the beginning of a composition, at the change of episodes, and also for the continual equalizing of the form of the whole work, without which the music would be reduced to immobility or to an amorphous fluidity, to which it is inclined by reason of its essentially contemplative nature and its perpetual rubato. Contemplative immobility and shapeless fluidity are the sources from which this music emanated and to which it always returns in a poor performance. But to provide against this there is the rhythm. The rhythm in Debussy's compositions has a self-sufficing, primordial significance. In it is the whole compositive essence of his music. For a very long time the erroneous opinion existed — and it still exists — that Debussy's music is not rhythmical. This mistake is due to an inaccurate comprehension of the parts played by metre and rhythm in his compositions. The music may not be metrical, but it is very rhythmical. It is more rhapsodical than any other, but it is not improvisational — a fact which is overlooked.

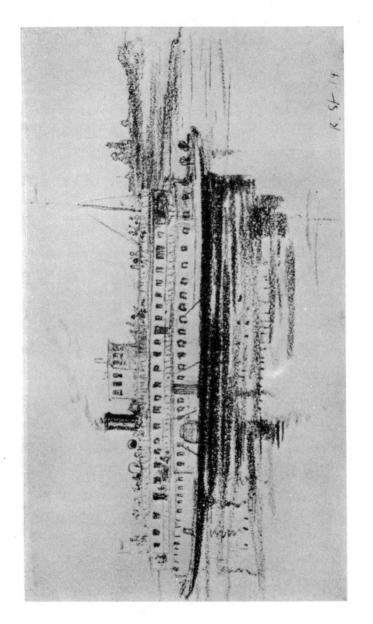

THE BOAT of the Third Volga Tour in 1914 — by ROBERT STERL

Debussy has done most interesting things with the metrical forms. He has been eminently successful in freeing musical rhythm from the dependence on metre — a dependence which has always existed as though it were unalterable, almost like the law of gravitation. Having liberated rhythm from the schematism of metre, Debussy used it as a foundation on which to build. Rhythm, understood as the structure of the elements of a composition, as the organization of its tonal particles, was developed by Debussy with a persistence found only among masters of the very highest order. He protected himself with the aid of the compositive role of rhythm, instinctively and un-consciously (unlike some of his contemporaries), from the dissolution of the material and the aridity to which impressionism, as a system of composition, led. The impressionist method does not result in a musical composition, but in a wandering about among static resonances which flare up and die down and, like will-o'-the-wisps, entice the wayfarer into the morass, so to speak, where he is eventually swallowed up. . . .

But for Debussy's healthy instinct for self-

protection nothing of his music would have remained
— it would have perished together with his period. All
the fruits of impressionism as a school testify to this,
particularly the leaders of the movement at the present day, who have been poisoned by the mephitic
vapours rising from the depths of the impressionist
morass. Meanwhile Debussy's music has outgrown its
time and come through safe and sound. The infelicity
perceptible in it is explained, not by the viciousness
of the impressionist method, which the power of
Debussy's creative will enabled him to overcome,
but by the general crisis sufficiently evident in his
day. It might be described as the Latin decadence,
and it found very pungent expression in Debussy's
music. . . .

Returning to Koussevitzky's concerts, we thus see
that the St. Petersburg and Moscow period of his
activities was pre-eminently western European. It
made itself effective in the dissemination of the
classics, mainly German, on the one hand, and
on the other it propagated and familiarized people
with the new music, preferably French. The French
classical composers and representatives of Ger-

man modernism also found a place in Koussevitzky's programs, but their inclusion was merely
incidental.

The symphonic literature of the French classical
masters is very soon exhausted and, moreover, ap-
peals to the tastes of the lover of rarities rather than
to the general public. The products of German modernism in the early years of the twentieth century
seemed crude and clumsy in comparison with the
highly spiced productions of their French confreres,
who concocted the most dainty and piquant dishes.
For the Germanic countries this was the period of
Richard Strauss's blooming; in Germany and Austria
there was even a sort of Richard Strauss cult. His
works appeared fairly often on Koussevitzky's programs. Koussevitzky performed them very readily,
and this is comprehensible in view of the fact that
they provide a conductor with an extremely grateful
part. All the same, appearances were to the contrary. They did not love Strauss in Russia. I have
in mind, of course, the advanced group of Russian
musicians, since the conservative circles in general
were not fond of anything and could not distinguish

Strauss from Debussy. They adopted an attitude of fastidious aversion to everything new and locked themselves up in the profundity of a sublime ignorance.

The Russian modernists disliked Strauss on account of his coarseness and the indubitable presence of vulgar material in his music. He repelled them by his lack of discrimination in his choice of subjects, his pursuit of cheap and easy effects, and his contentment with the first musical material that came to hand. But in their antipathy, justifiable in many respects, they overlooked what was most valuable in Strauss, and what, in my view, immediately and with unquestionable clearness, speaks for itself. I refer to the quality of his instrumental writing. The facture of Strauss's orchestral works is magnificent. Based nearly always on very doubtful, at times very cheap, material, the facture of his writing is invariably full of the real essence of music. His instrumental thinking is superb, the construction is always solid, and the logic of his distribution of the parts convincing. His scores probably contain more opportunities for the display of instrumental virtuosity than any others written during the first quarter of the present century. In spite of his specific and exceptional virtuosity, Strauss is neither schematic nor formal. If he had been able to put aside his æsthetic and programmatic predilections and the bad taste prevailing in his compositions — by no means an easy matter — we should have before us a creative force of the highest order. But it must not be forgotten that his is an exclusively virtuoso art. In this is its defect and at the same time its merit. The technique of this music is a separate thing by itself, and so is the spiritual and material content with which it is filled. Given another culture and different tastes, the virtuoso technique might have been applied to other purposes.

Till Eulenspiegel, Don Juan, and *Zarathustra* were often given by Koussevitzky.

The lines on which Koussevitzky as a conductor proceeded at this period seem to me to have been well defined and in accord with the times. I doubt if this was the outcome of any considered plan; more probably he was guided by an instinctive gravitation towards this or the other category of musical works, as is natural to every genuine artist, but we now see that he made no mistakes, nor followed false trails. What part did he play in connexion with Russian music as such?

From my exposition of events it may seem that he avoided it and was entirely absorbed in the music, classical or modern, of western Europe. This impression would be incorrect; Koussevitzky did not overlook Russian music, but performed it side by side with the other. In his concerts at that time he brought forward the best works produced by the official Russian musicians of the day: Rimsky-Korsakov, Taneiev, Glazounov, Lyadov, and others. I will not confine myself to a dreary enumeration of the compositions played by him, but will endeavour to deduce the fundamental lines along which it may be possible to trace the development of Russian music at that period, surveying it in its historical aspect. I am bound to say, however, that these deductions of mine are by no means binding on anyone and merely represent my personal views.

During these years the official Russian music found itself at the cross-roads. What remained of the national school — the " mighty band " — was only a heritage. Its tendencies and activities had been stabilized. The school as such was already liquidated and proved to be firmly bound up with official musical education, whose fate was in the hands of the Russian Musical Society — that is, the Conservatory and the society's concerts.

In actual fact this stabilization had begun far earlier — from the moment that Balakirev's role was replaced by Rimsky-Korsakov's authority. The living spirit ceased to exist in this sphere. Creative work became academic, with conservative tendencies in every direction. It was pre-eminently a belated repetition of the songs that western Europe had sung a quarter of a century earlier. If these people's retrospective glance had extended further back than twenty-five years, it would, of course, have been all the better. As for the education emanating from academicism of such a nature, it was governed by schematic and abstract principles, which were set forth in the formulas of a futile scholasticism, adapted to turn the young student into an unemotional craftsman and not to train his creative powers. Nevertheless this educational method saved a whole generation from the unruliness which made its appearance simultaneously with modernism. Later on, it broke out in the form of anarchy over nearly the whole of Europe, and if Russia was exempt at that time, it was only because the craftsman's discipline acquired on the school benches held many in a grip of iron.

Koussevitzky had nothing to do with this circle. He had nothing in common with opera, on which the work of the national school was mainly based and in which it achieved its greatest triumphs. Though frequently invited to conduct there, he never chose to accept.

Moussorgsky's creations — the supreme achievement and the richest treasures of the national school during the existence of the " mighty band " — were all but placed on the index and underwent plumbing and painting by Rimsky-Korsakov's heirs and the musicians of his clan. Any attempt to restore Moussorgsky's features to their original condition, to let us see them as they were before Rimsky-Korsakov touched them up, met with furious opposition, and if any such dare-devil belonged to the Rimsky-Korsakov circle, he was practically outlawed. Not until the revolution were the first steps taken towards the rehabilitation of the real Moussorgsky.

Nationalism in Russian music was, on the whole, out of fashion in those days. It might be possible to mention a few men who had serious and intelligent ideas concerning the national problem of the Russian musical art. Their views on the subject differed from those held in official musical circles and were entirely free from any dependence on the culture of western Europe.

The most prominent of the young and advanced composers at that time was Stravinsky, who was then a long way from the position which he subsequently occupied. After the creation of *Petrushka* and *The Rite of Spring* he obtained a place in the front rank of European and Russian composers, although the true significance of what he was doing and of the part he was playing was not realized then. Koussevitzky conducted the first concert-performance in Russia of *The Rite of Spring* in its entirety in 1913 and was the first to give *Petrushka*. It was not the ballet version he gave, but a concert suite — that is, " Russian Dance," " Scene at Petrushka's," and " The Fair."

Koussevitzky called this suite *Fragments from "Petrushka."* This material was afterwards worked up by Stravinsky for piano solo, under the title of *Three Movements from "Petrushka."*

Myaskovsky, amongst other young composers, was introduced to the public by Koussevitzky, who played his orchestral composition *Alastor* for the first time.

As we are confining ourselves to a survey of the most fundamental and important aspects of the development of Russian music, I will leave aside the question of the significance of the work accomplished by the leaders of the national school. In my opinion it was a valuable contribution to musical culture, but was of second-rate quality. Whilst paying due tribute to the creations of such masters as Rimsky-Korsakov, Taneiev, Glazounov, and Lyadov, I do not think I shall be detracting from their importance to Russian music as a whole, nor depreciating the part they played in it, if I assert that, so far as the Russian symphonic music of that period is concerned, only two men count — Tchaikovsky and Scriabin.

Koussevitsky had already shown his apprecia-

SERGEI KOUSSEVITZKY and A. SCRIABIN
as soloist in his piano concerto during the Volga Tour in 1910
by ROBERT STERL

tion of Tchaikovsky to the fullest extent possible under the existing conditions, which were determined by the attitude of Russian musical circles towards this great musician.

As for Scriabin, Koussevitzky was more closely connected with him than with any other composer of that period, and their names were destined to be inseparably and organically linked together in the history of Russian music.

CHAPTER ELEVEN

From Tchaikovsky to Scriabin

TWENTY YEARS AGO ANYONE IN THE FULL POSSESSION
of his powers required a great deal of courage to
confess that he admired Tchaikovsky. In modernist
circles such an admission would have been regarded
as a sign of bad taste. The public — in Russia as in
Europe, with the exception of France — has never
ceased to love Tchaikovsky and has invariably been
faithful to him, in bygone times as well as now. The
attitude of the public is a different matter; it has

always appreciated Tchaikovsky's lyricism and emotional pathos rather than his musical merits, which it has hardly observed or understood. It is only by his passionate, almost morbid temperament that he has impressed the crowd. But for that his music would have been as far beyond the listener's reach as Mozart's or Glinka's. A strange fate overtook Tchaikovsky. He was one of the most distinguished musicians of the nineteenth century — and this was beyond debate even for those who were unquestionably hostile to him. Moreover, he was the only symphonist in Russian music until Scriabin arrived; upon him the burden of the symphonic musical element devolved, and in this respect he was almost equal to Beethoven.

In speaking of symphonism I do not refer to the mere composition of music for the orchestra, even very successful music, but to a peculiar spiritual emanation, a state of spiritual tenseness, expressed by the composer in the purely instrumental sphere. (It may not be necessary to explain this, but I prefer to do so rather than run the risk of possible misunderstandings in regard to terminology.) Therefore any kind of program or descriptive music — music applied to subjects which are outside itself — is not symphonism, even though written for a symphony orchestra.

The music of Bach, Mozart, Beethoven, Brahms, and Tchaikovsky may be described as the supreme expression of pure symphonism. Much else might be included under the term, but always with reservations.

So, then, Tchaikovsky was appreciated and lauded to the skies by the man in the street, but never received recognition from the professional musicians, who, with rare exceptions, treated his music with fastidious irony. During his lifetime he was disliked by the members of the " mighty band," then in the forefront of Russian music, on account of his " Westernism," his sympathies with Latin culture, his fondness for the Italians and for certain of the Frenchmen. To the composers of the national school he seemed to be almost a foreigner. They could find no grounds for regarding his music as Russian. We now know very well how mistaken they all were.

Balakirev was wrong and so was Rimsky-Korsakov, but not Tchaikovsky. The national school considered that they were the direct successors of Glinka and were carrying on his work — in this consisted their fundamental problem. Tchaikovsky had no problem except his life of torture.

When the light of history, however, is thrown upon the question, it becomes incontestably evident that Tchaikovsky is the only composer having a direct, vital, creative, and not problematical connexion with Glinka, and that the musicians of Balakirev's circle had turned aside into an entirely different path from Glinka's.

Later, in the era of modernism, the modernists began to despise Tchaikovsky, and this was carried on even more impudently than before. Since then to dislike Tchaikovsky has become almost a tradition and is considered quite natural, not only by the modernists, but also by the ordinary members of the intelligentsia, who were once particularly drawn to him, since they had an idea that he stimulated the "civic sorrow."

When, some years ago, Stravinsky came forward in Europe as a defender of Tchaikovsky, he caused a certain amount of uneasiness. This, however, very quickly subsided, and on the whole things have remained pretty much as they were, except that certain persons knowing that a revaluation of Tchaikovsky has taken place are now, through cowardice, afraid to admit that they cannot endure his music, " *et ils font bonne mine au mavais jeu. . . .*"

This is not the place to dwell upon this question, but a few words will suffice to explain the attitude towards Tchaikovsky and to show us that there are no riddles and nothing wonderful about it.

Tchaikovsky never was an innovator or a revolutionary in art. He was simply a very fine musician. Notwithstanding the exceptional, almost hysterical morbidness which was natural to him and which he introduced into his art, his music is of itself entirely normal. It is extraordinarily normal, and that is the only reason why those who always want the unusual dislike it. To the man who is not fond of the normal it seems dreadfully commonplace and insipid. Tchaikovsky's music does not interest the gourmand, does not attract him or stimulate his appetite. He always finds it very difficult to take in normal professionalism in art, particularly if it is normalized to such a degree that it falls little short of perfection.

The mistake of most conductors in performing Tchaikovsky is that they stress his hysterical morbidness, thrusting it into the foreground and ransacking it — probing its vitals, as it were — and allowing nothing else to be seen or heard. This side of his art should be tactfully suppressed, just as we conceal the malady of a friend instead of advertising it to the whole world. If this is achieved, Tchaikovsky's music speaks for itself and reveals a wealth of incomparable beauties. It is true that this makes it far more difficult to grasp, but it is the only way to arrive at the real Tchaikovsky. Failing this, everything remains as before; that is to say, he is used as profitable and easily yielding material with which to play upon the nerves and evil instincts of the crowd, thus justifying the opinion of those who consider that art of such a kind can be pleasing only to people of very bad taste.

In his interpretation of Tchaikovsky Koussevitzky proceeded by stages. This composer was very close to his heart. He loved him, and played him from time to time at different periods. The modernists shut their eyes to the fact that Koussevitzky played Tchaikovsky, but nobody could pay any serious attention to that. They imagined that he did it to please the public, to advance his own success; and they condescendingly forgave him, as one forgives the whims of a prima donna. In thinking thus they were very wide of the mark. Koussevitzky's relations with Tchaikovsky had nothing to do with modernism, but were really due to Nikisch, who was passionately fond of Tchaikovsky and was at that time his best interpreter.

At this period Koussevitzky also based his performances of Tchaikovsky on the emotional side of the music. Then for a long time he forsook Tchaikovsky, to whom he has only recently returned, after undergoing a great and serious evolution. He has now adopted a correct and entirely new method of treating this composer. It is very interesting to observe how Koussevitzky's evolution has cleared away the obstacles which for ten years have blocked the path to Tchaikovsky. Koussevitzky is the first to show him to us as we ought to see him, regardless of the fact that in so doing he may perplex many and scare them away. His action in this matter will compel audiences and performers alike to break with the bad habits to which they have become inured.

A historical perspective of Russian music over a long stretch of time — from the last decade of the nineteenth century to the present day — will show us that Scriabin is in the direct line of descent from Tchaikovsky, and that the former was succeeded by Stravinsky. Scriabin had nothing in common with Tchaikovsky, towards whom he adopted a very haughty attitude; Stravinsky feels precisely the same about Scriabin, but finds that he has a close affinity with Tchaikovsky, which he cherishes and cultivates. Thus the two widely separated generations are drawn to each other, whilst the intervening link is passed over.

It is interesting to note that all three are "Westerners." Stravinsky began as a keen exponent of nationalism, got past this, and became an even more zealous apostle of "Westernism" than were Tchaikovsky and Scriabin. It is a curious and almost paradoxical fact that Debussy was the only non-Westerner at the beginning of the twentieth century. . . .

Beyond question a tie does exist between Scriabin and Tchaikovsky. Ten years ago I wrote concerning this: " The further we get away from the past of

Russian music, the nearer do Scriabin and Tchaikovsky approach each other — the antipodes, closely akin in their polarity, and in Russian music the sole possessors of the musical element, of the spirit of music."

Again, in April 1920, in my speech at the Scriabin functions held in Moscow on the fifth anniversary of his death, I said: " Scriabin and Tchaikovsky are two stages of Russian symphonism, the antipodes of each other in temperament and outlook. The self-forgetfulness of the one carries him to ecstatic rapture, to the limits of audacity; the self-forgetfulness of the other to anguish and self-annihilation. Opposite poles, both are profoundly characteristic of the nature of the Russian artistic temperament. To an equal extent they were mouthpieces of the Russian intelligentsia — Tchaikovsky spoke for the intelligentsia of the seventies and eighties, while Scriabin expressed the artistic ideals of the Russian intelligentsia of his day.

" This may explain the direct emotional reaction of Scriabin on the crowd, on his hearers. Even when the majority of the specialists were bitterly hostile to him and disavowed him, the Russian intelligentsia accepted him ardently and unconditionally."

I permit myself these quotations because I imagine that my feelings on the subject were correct at the time and that they did not deceive me. For the last ten years of his life Scriabin was idolized by the young Russian musicians. His compositions and his gifts as a pianist were equally prized. In both departments of the musical art he had been endowed with the captivating power of charm. Beyond this he had nothing, just as he was without a trace of professional authority. But the power of his charm was veritably unlimited. This, the true Orphic enchantment, will never be forgotten by those who heard him. The naïve crudity of his " æsthetic," the hazy, semi-delirious literary prefaces to his compositions, his false " mystics," have departed into the past, never to return. The only purpose they served was to provide him with a motive for his creative work. But the musical vestiges of the ardour and enthusiasm of his soul will for ever remain indelible. Scriabin was one of the last of those artists for whom the spirit of music was the spirit of humanistic culture. This ceased to be so after him,

and for a long time art has lost its humanistic significance and has devoted itself to entirely different aims.

During those years when modernism was in its
prime, Russia turned with Scriabin to the West, with
its face towards Europe, whereas Europe, led by Debussy, addressed itself to the East — that is, to Russia.
In the consequences arising from this we have the
whole meaning of the historical process in musical
art at the beginning of the twentieth century.

When in St. Petersburg in 1921, at a meeting of
the Free Philosophical Association I read a paper in
which I tried to formulate the problems of musical art
in their historical aspect, so far as a historical estimate
in regard to the heritage bequeathed by Scriabin and
Debussy was then possible. The period during which
they had been the leaders of the new movement in
music had only just come to an end, and their creative
work was still a living force.

I wrote as follows: " Scriabin and Debussy were
at the opposite poles of the music contemporary with
our pre-revolutionary period, the former being the
typical representative of the culture of western Europe, and the latter the most powerful exponent of the

culture of the East. We know now that Debussyism as a school stood for the revival of national French music and for the liberation of French music from the ascendancy of Wagner's ideas, to which it had long been subjected. Debussy restored to it the purity of its instrumental style and freed it from the influence of the pseudo-monumental forms of the German music of the late nineteenth century. In the last period of his activities Debussy achieved the rehabilitation of the national traditions of French music; in his instrumental works he established a living bond with the French clavecinists of the eighteenth century, whilst his vocal compositions took him back, through the poetry of the Middle Ages, to the music of the thirteenth-century troubadours. On his way he abandoned for a long period the whole of the musical culture of western Europe and immersed himself in the art of the East. Here, in this baptismal font, under the powerful effects of Chinese and Japanese painting, but mainly through the direct influence of Russian music — the orthodox Byzantine canticles, the national folksong, the compositions of Moussorgsky — was accomplished the regeneration of French music, the outward sign of which was a decided reaction against the western European music of the nineteenth century. Thus Debussy's creative journeyings ended in a sort of Scythian incursion on Latin culture.

"Debussy, that genius of the most refined tastes, had to assume the attitude of a barbarian when he broke with the past in order to restore the purity of French music on a national basis. For this purpose he invented new forms in which to incarnate it, a new language of the feelings, a new tonal outlook, and connected his own times with the original traditions of bygone cultures, forgotten and smothered with the weeds which had sprung up on the paths of art at the end of the nineteenth century.

"In Scriabin's case the process was reversed. Striving from the very first to escape from the narrow, restricted circle of Russian national music and the forms by which it was fettered in those days, he at once adopted as the sole basis of his creative work the contemporary musical culture of western Europe and broke decisively with the Russian music of the past in all its aspects. Underlying his creations we find everything that characterized western European music in the last years of the nineteenth century — we find Schumann, Chopin, Liszt, Wagner. Scriabin suppressed the vocal side of his nature in favour of the purely instrumental. He obtained his ' liberation,' not by consciously overcoming the false traditions of Russian music, but by a direct and deliberate rupture with all its ways. He got away from the traditional folk-lore aspect of Russian music and the traditional forms in which it was embodied in his day, but he did not discover the pure instrumental principles fundamental to the nature of Russian music, as he had at the same time fallen under the influence of the then effete cultural and ideological traditions of western European music. He could not find a foothold in pure music. He tried to obtain one by means of his emotional inspiration, on the bases of his original, occult, æsthetico-philosophical ideology, which predetermined his emotionalism. Hence arose Scriabin's schematism, created by him when he committed to writing his ideological programmatic conceptions; hence this schematism, peculiar to him, is almost as self-circumscribed and catastrophic, and for the coming generations as doomed, as the schematism of Russian music in its traditional form, since we have here no possibility of the organic development of the musical forms and material — as past years have shown."

After a lapse of ten years I have nothing to add to this, except, perhaps, that the problem of the material relations of the two cultures — the Eastern and the Western — has since been solved by Stravinsky, on entirely different lines from Scriabin's, without any æsthetico-mystical ideology and under other conditions. In his creations he has taken Russian music out of the narrow sphere of nationalism and treated it from a universal standpoint. That which was for Scriabin the tormenting and tragical memory of his life has become for Stravinsky, in the altered circumstances of our time, an exclusively professional matter and a problem of a purely formal order.

The organic synthesis of two different musical cultures which was created by Glinka and became the foundation of Russian music — the synthesis which Rimsky-Korsakov endeavoured unsuccessfully and mechanically to revive and continue — has been achieved in our time by the genius of Stravinsky, under different conditions and by other means. It is,

FIRST PERFORMANCE OF *PROMETHEUS*
IN MOSCOW — by PASTERNACK

however, too early to formulate any categorical infer-
ences and conclusions in regard to it.

In the person of Koussevitzky Scriabin encountered, in the literal sense of the word, an interpreter
in entire sympathy with his compositions. It is impossible to imagine anything happier or more successful
than the combination of these two temperaments.
If Scriabin had been as fine an orchestral conductor
as he was a pianist, he could not have performed
his orchestral works better than Koussevitzky did.

Koussevitzky's treatment of this music was not of
the usual order; it was not even merely a superb display of professional skill. It was a kind of musical
inspiration and an " act." It was what the music became when the composer himself played it at the
piano.

When Koussevitzky performed Scriabin's symphonies, the *Poem of Ecstasy* and *Prometheus* ceased
to be musical works in the proper sense of the term
and rose to such a high level of tenseness and creative
saturation that their " professional " character was
completely dissolved away and an impression of almost "noumenal " music produced. In contact with

the audience it set up the cleansing process known to the ancient Greeks as " catharsis." . . .

In the last year of Scriabin's life a rupture took place between him and Koussevitzky, concerning which many and various explanations have been put forward. I think the reason must be sought not so much in the surroundings as in circumstances of a more substantial nature.

It seems to me that a contributing cause was the fact that Koussevitzky's artistic horizons were not circumscribed by Scriabin, in spite of the exceptionally close musical contact existing between them. Koussevitzky could not become a fanatical devotee of Scriabin's ideology. Notwithstanding his passionate attachment to Scriabin's music at that time, he did not develop into an idolator of Scriabinism, a kind of heresy, almost of a pseudo-religious nature, with which Scriabin's familiar friends were infected. In his relations with Scriabin Koussevitzky always had a rationalistic power of resistance, whereby he protected himself from the chaos and extravagances into which the former was drawn. The absolute pathos of striving for one idea was not an attribute of Koussevitzky's, wherefore he could not at that time become a Scriabin fanatic — and this was indispensable to the maintenance of a close contact with the composer. Koussevitzky loves art as a whole and reconciles in himself its various manifestations. It may be supposed that if in his time he had become Scriabinist to the nth degree, his activities would have ended with that period and he would have been incapable of anything further. In resisting Scriabin Koussevitzky was protecting his own future, and it may be that to this alone he owes the continuation of his musical career.

CHAPTER TWELVE

The War

KOUSSEVITZKY'S CONCERT SEASON OF 1914–15 WAS
carried on entirely under war conditions. Soon after
the outbreak of hostilities he gave a benefit concert —
the first of its kind — at Sokolniki, near Moscow, the
whole of the proceeds being devoted to the relief of
the wives of soldiers at the front. For the first time the
national anthems of Russia's allies were played. During the performance of the Russian hymn Koussevitzky turned to the audience, some eight thousand in

number, with the suggestion that they should join in
the singing. It was an inspiring spectacle, and the
sound of the many voices blending with the orchestra
aroused the enthusiasm of all who were present at this
heroic moment. . . . Henceforth it became a tradition that the national hymns of the allies should be
played throughout the war at theatres and concerts
all over Russia.

On the whole this first war-time season was fairly
successful, but in the season of 1915–16 serious
troubles arose and a decline set in. To begin with,
Koussevitzky had to transfer his concerts to the theatres, as the halls of the Nobles' Clubs in Moscow and
St. Petersburg were occupied as hospitals for the
wounded. Then there was great difficulty in conveying
the orchestra from one capital to the other, the trains
being needed for the transport of civil and military
supplies. Under these conditions they made the journey once a month only, instead of twice, and gave two
concerts during the fortnight. Nearly all the other concert societies had by then ceased operations. Koussevitzky displayed extraordinary energy and persistence, as he was reluctant to give in, even while the war

was on, and thereby bring to an end the work he had
so soundly organized. The opinion was formed that he
would carry on under any conditions, even the most
desperate. If all the premises in St. Petersburg and
Moscow were taken over by the military organizations,
he would go into the cellars rather than discontinue
the concerts.

In addition to the disorder in the administration,
symptoms of a far more alarming nature now made
their appearance, and they interfered with the concerts much more seriously than the practical and
technical deficiencies created by the war. A false
patriotism, with an ugly meaning, sprang up side by
side with a lofty and genuinely patriotic and national
ardour.

People tuned up to the proper pitch attacked German music, demanding its exclusion from concert
programs. This foolish and fictitious " patriotism "
brought about an utterly impossible state of things
and was intolerable to anyone possessed of a modicum
of common sense. A proposal to ostracize only contemporary German music might have been more or
less comprehensible, but the whole of German classi-

cism was to be brought under the ban as well — Beethoven, Mozart, Haydn, Bach, etc.

German " patriots " of this order conducted themselves similarly in their country. I recollect the disturbances caused by the performance of Debussy in Berlin concert halls several years after the conclusion of peace, in 1922.

Koussevitzky received " patriotic " letters from writers of this type, threatening to suppress him if he continued to play Beethoven. It should be said that he took no notice of them and went on with his work, putting Beethoven on his programs despite the threats, but it became increasingly difficult to carry on the concerts.

He had displayed his courage on previous occasions, taking his own line regardless of obstacles which were thrown in his way by hostile forces. A case in point is the political demonstration which took place at his concert in connexion with the death of Lëv Tolstoi. This was in 1911. Already the social and national revolt, which broke out as the revolutionary element in 1917, was coming to a head.

Tolstoi died estranged from the Church and

morally persecuted by the State. The police took measures to prevent any demonstration of the social feeling in connexion with the death, which was an occasion for national mourning in Russia. A Koussevitzky concert was held in St. Petersburg a few days after the event.

When Koussevitzky appeared on the platform, he gave the signal to the orchestra, who rose and were followed by the audience. In an atmosphere of solemn silence they stood thus for a minute, after which, at a sign from Koussevitzky, they resumed their seats, and the concert began. This demonstration made a great impression. It was expected that Koussevitzky would hardly escape exile, and as a matter of fact he received a communication on the following day from the Governor of St. Petersburg demanding an explanation. On what grounds, it was asked, did he hold this demonstration without the sanction of the authorities. Under the political régime existing in those days it was a great piece of daring. Koussevitzky pointed out that no speeches were made at the demonstration, and explained that he considered it indispensable to honour the memory of a great artist. The occurrence had no further consequences.

Koussevitzky had personal recollections of Tolstoi. He once visited him at Yasnaya Polyana with the Société des Instruments Anciens. Koussevitzky played the double-bass. Tolstoi, a passionate lover of music, received the musicians cordially and was touched by the attention paid him. The visitors have preserved unforgettable memories of the figure of the great writer.

In the spring of 1915 Koussevitzky took his orchestra to south Russia, where he gave six concerts, the proceeds of which were set apart for war charities. Rachmaninoff was the soloist at these concerts.

Scriabin died in the spring of 1915, suddenly and tragically, at the height of his powers, without having realized even a fragmentary portion of the grandiose plans with which he was brimming over. His family were left without the means of subsistence, and Koussevitzky gave a cycle of his orchestral and pianoforte compositions for their benefit. Rachmaninoff, Orlov, Borovsky, and others took part in the concerts as soloists. For the same purpose Koussevitzky returned to his instrument after a long interval and gave a double-bass recital.

A memory of that evening has been preserved in an impromptu poem in honour of Koussevitzky written by the poet Balmont at the concert, under the impressions produced by his playing, and read by the poet from the platform:

To S. A. Koussevitzky Playing the Double-Bass

I know that today I have seen a great wonder:
A sacred scarab sang and droned;
A clear call came from where the thunder
Ripens midst surging clouds — and echoed
In my soul. But, suddenly, the singing scarab
Changed to a gliding boat,
Its slender oar flashed white,
Then strings vibrated with music sibyl-like
And, glowing, woke the heart alike.
But, he, the wizard, with both his hands,
Showers a rain of melody upon us
And all aflame, with fingers trembling,
Touching the strings, touched every heart,
In its response, the strings resembling.

In 1916 more than half of Koussevitzky's players were called to the war. This brought about the final collapse of the orchestra and put an end to its existence. But the concerts still went on in the season of 1916–17. He gave them in St. Petersburg and Moscow with the remains of his orchestra, supplemented by musicians from the bands of the Imperial Theatres. In January 1917 he travelled Russia as a soloist and gave twenty double-bass recitals. This took the place of the American tour which had been proposed to him some time before the war. It was to have taken place in 1916–17, and he was to appear in the double capacity of conductor and soloist. He had accepted the offer and signed the contract prior to the outbreak of hostilities, but 1914 put a stop to it. The blockade and the difficulties of travel made him even alter his plans for a tour through Japan. In America his impending arrival was announced and his concerts advertised. Everything was ready for his departure, and the railway tickets were taken. But the war threw obstacles in his way, and the journey came to nothing.

The revolution occurred in February 1917; the elements broke loose, demolishing all Koussevitzky's plans and radically changing all his surroundings and the conditions under which he existed.

CHAPTER THIRTEEN

The Revolution

Of the Russian Revolution much has been written. A vast literature on the subject has already been created by writers belonging to various grades of the Russian social scale and to every class and order, connected with different social circles and professing political convictions ranging from the extreme right to the extreme left. But all this is, of course, in the mean time only material for the future, very rich and circumstantial material, it is true, except in one

section, in which a great gap exists. That section is —
art. Those who belonged to one or other of the art
circles in Russia, on joining the ranks of the émigrés,
wrote of the revolution from an almost entirely commonplace point of view, and though this may be
dramatic, it is none the less commonplace.

We have not sufficient material to enable us to
form an objective estimate of the perversion of Russian art in general, and of music in particular, which
has taken place as a result of the social revolution,
and such as we have is of a one-sided character and
narrow in its outlook. For one who, like the author
of these lines, was not a passive observer of what was
happening, but an active participant in the process,
the evidence concerning those times must be a subject
for individual investigation. . . . Later on I may be
able to devote a special work to my reminiscences of
that period, in which I shall deal with my musical
activities in connexion with it and explain, from my
point of view, the nature of the mutual relations established between art workers and the authorities in
the earliest days of the revolution, and the effect of the
revolution itself on the artistic culture of the country.

The investigation to which I have referred may be undertaken at some future date, but I must confine myself here to a cursory glance at Koussevitzky's experiences during those tragic years.

The maturing of the revolutionary plans which culminated in the explosion of 1917 was a long and painful process. It became evident then that the imperial power, upon which the old régime still relied, had definitely crumbled. About that time all that was in any way meritorious in the conservative circles of monarchical Russia held aloof from the contemporary despotic régime, which was maintained solely by the power wielded by unprincipled bureaucrats and careerist officials. Where any vitality existed, it was gasping for breath in the stifling atmosphere created by the Government. The whole country welcomed the revolution of 1917 with a sigh of relief, with enthusiasm and acclamation. All who were not inseparably shackled to the official bureaucracy saw in the revolution a liberating element, which set free the vital forces of the country and brought life and restoration to those who had been gripped in the clutches of reaction and despotism.

In the interregnum between the destruction of the monarchy and the dictatorship of the proletariat the power passed from the bureaucracy and the higher officials to the liberal bourgeoisie and the qualified intelligentsia, who were masters of the situation from February to October 1917. But in the conditions of the revolution the process of state reorganization was not systematic: it began from the very first to assume an elemental and impetuous character, restrained as far as possible by the moderate rather than the revolutionary principles of the new Government.

The revolution also introduced changes into the artistic life of the country. The new Government dismissed the functionaries and called in the important artists of its own circle to administer matters affecting art and to carry out its intended reforms. Koussevitzky, who occupied a foremost place in Russian musical life, was the first to be invited. At the beginning of May 1917 he received a letter from N. F. Golovin (formerly president of the eleventh Imperial Duma), who had been appointed by the revolutionary authorities to take charge of the establishments (including the theatres) previously under the jurisdiction of the Ministry of the Court.

The letter ran as follows:

Commissar of the Temporary Government over the former Ministry of the Court and Apanages

Dear Sergei Alexandrovitch:

The great historical events which have recently occurred, involving radical changes in the organization of our State, have brought forward, side by side with the uplifting of all the social forces and tendencies, a series of new problems in every branch of our national creative work.

Wide circles of the people, hitherto deprived of the possibility of coming into direct contact with art, and particularly with music, have a right to be, and should be, brought within reach of it. In this respect a prominent part might be played by the former Court Orchestra and Chapel, which have until now been restricted to the service of the Court of the late Tsar, and which I propose should now become the State Symphony Orchestra and Chapel. Both these establishments, having considerable musical forces at their disposal, appear to be artistic units of considerable strength, but they need thorough reorganization to fit them for their new and exalted tasks. Such reorganization could be achieved only if con-

trolled by someone whose authority would be generally recognized, who is an ardent lover of the art, and who, thanks to his talent, would be able to establish contact with the people and get the best out of them.

Knowing you and profoundly appreciating your gifts, I am firmly persuaded that you could successfully cope with the tasks imposed upon us at the present time, and I beg you not to refuse to undertake them — it is a supremely noble work, though by no means an easy one. Confident that all details can be easily arranged at a personal interview, I shall be very much obliged if, in the event of your accepting in principle, you will come to Petrograd as soon as possible.

Please accept the assurance of my profound esteem and devotion.

Golovin

No. 1494
8 May 1917

Koussevitzky accepted the commission so far as the ci-devant Court Orchestra was concerned, but declined to undertake the direction of the Chapel. In connexion with the former, serious difficulties at once arose. Prior to the revolution the work of the orchestra from an artistic point of view was of little value. Its duties were to play at court during breakfast and dinner and at official receptions or evening parties. Its appearances before the general public were limited to a series of semi-popular matinées. There was no real discipline. The musicians were accustomed to taking things easy and to the privileged position conferred upon them by their service under the Ministry of the Court. There were some fine players among them, but in order to put the whole orchestra on a sound footing and to obtain strict discipline and real artistic work radical changes were necessary. First and foremost the musty atmosphere of their surroundings, due to the Ministry of the Court, had to be dissipated and a thorough reorganization of the orchestra on new and normal lines, in preparation for serious work, taken in hand. In actual fact Koussevitzky did not succeed in accomplishing this, for many reasons. In the first place, he was not an official, but an artist and too important a conductor for this orchestra. Then, in proportion as the revolutionary element grew and strengthened, the material conditions connected with the existence of the orchestra deteriorated, until they became excessively onerous. As it was impossible to guarantee their salaries, even within the most modest limits, Koussevitzky could not exact a high standard of art from his musicians nor enforce a rigid discipline. He had to devote more of his time to smoothing over the endless troubles connected with the delays in the payment of their salaries than to purely artistic matters.

Having accepted the responsibility of managing the orchestra, he always and invariably took a keen interest in everything affecting it. He used his official position on its behalf in dealing with the authorities, and his moral support helped the members to keep up their courage at the most difficult period of the revolution.

Koussevitzky gave a series of concerts with this orchestra. Though few in number, they were of exceptional value, and in the conditions then prevailing were important events for art and the public. They provided a few moments of forgetfulness amidst the tragic surroundings created by the revolution. The last of these concerts took place in a hall at the Nobles' Club, Petrograd, which was filled to overflowing. Shortly afterwards, in the spring of 1920, Koussevitzky left Russia.

The State Orchestra may not have attained the perfection reached by Koussevitzky's own organization, but he improved it as far as possible in the circumstances and, what was most important, co-operated in saving it from disbandment. After his departure abroad, it was transformed into the Petrograd Philharmonic and has become the basis of the musical life of Leningrad.

Though he had undertaken the conductorship of the State Orchestra, Koussevitzky did not discontinue his private concert work. At the beginning of the revolution he devoted himself to it with enthusiasm and renewed energy, as the first revolution revealed new horizons to him and widened the sphere of his activity. The idea of appearing before a vast popular audience appealed to him. In May 1917 he arranged a people's concert in the Moscow circus, which was attended by about fifteen thousand people. By his invitation the eminent poets Balmont, Andrei Bely, Baltrushaitis, and Voloshin took part in the program, reading their verses for a popular audience between the musical items.

In Petrograd Koussevitzky appeared with the

horrified that he should have arrived at such a moment and advised him to return to Petrograd, as it
was impossible to drive through the streets of Moscow,
on account of the firing. The Bolshevist rising, which
was already over in Petrograd, had only just reached
Moscow. Koussevitzky was undecided as to what he
should do, but, being unwilling to leave his wife alone
at such a time, he determined to make an attempt to
get to his home. With difficulty he found a cabman
who was prepared to take him across the city. The
streets through which they passed were deserted, and
the whole place seemed to be dead. Now and then,
through the crack in the half-closed shutters, appeared
the nose of an inhabitant, who gazed with terror and
amazement at the man who dared to cross the city at
such an unseasonable time. Revolver shots and the
rattle of machine-guns resounded on all sides. . . .
They had accomplished half their journey when, in
one of the streets, they were hailed and ordered to
stop. Armed men surrounded the cab and asked
Koussevitzky if he had any weapons. He suddenly
remembered that he kept in his travelling dressing-
case a small revolver in a case; it had been given to

MOSCOW : Twerskoy Boulevard, by ROBERT STERL

him and he usually carried it about with him, but had quite forgotten its existence. When he told the men of it, one of them presented a revolver at his head and in a threatening tone demanded the surrender of the weapon. " You'll end by blowing my brains out," said Koussevitzky, with the coolness innate in him and characteristic of him in moments of danger. " Find my revolver first." They set to work to ransack his luggage, but no weapon was forthcoming. Koussevitzky found it and handed it over and then received permission to continue his journey. A little farther on they came under cross-fire. There seemed no possibility of reaching home. With firing everywhere and bullets whistling over their heads the situation was desperate, and it looked as though there was little prospect of their coming out alive. Seizing a favourable moment, Koussevitzky peremptorily ordered his cabman to drive at top speed, and they managed to cross the danger zone unharmed. They then got into a quiet side-street, where they found themselves in safety, and thenceforward there was no more trouble. On arriving at his home, he was met by Natalya Konstantinovna, much excited at his entirely unexpected

appearance, but happy to know that he had successfully escaped the dangers which had threatened him.

The overthrow of the bourgeois-intelligentsia re-
public made perhaps a greater impression on Russian
society than the fall of the monarchy. From the very
first, Koussevitzky was irreconcilably opposed to the
Soviet Government. As evidence of this I reproduce
the text of a letter published by him in the press in the
early days of the Soviet régime; in it he sets forth
the motives which induced him to continue his labours
under new rulers.

Letter to the Editor

*I ask you to find space in your esteemed news-
paper for the following statement.*

*In circles closely connected with the State
Orchestra and interested in its existence certain
persons have spread the report that I, who am
in command of the orchestra, am in full accord
with the Government of the " People's Commis-
sars." Furthermore, the fact that in the present
circumstances I continue to give concerts is held
by these persons to be a proof of my readiness to
come to terms with the " existing state of things "
— that is, to recognize it as lawful and normal.*

All this is entirely false. As I definitely stated

*in the course of the first few days after the recent
revolution, there can be no question of any " accord " between myself and the new Government;
like all sensible citizens, I shall submit only to
the government that shall be appointed by a con-
stituent assembly. Until then I shall remain in
charge of the State Orchestra, on the distinct understanding that no new " powers that be " shall
interfere in any way with its affairs.*

*In regard to the concerts, I shall continue to
give them, not, of course, to show my approval of
the harshest, most despotic and violent régime
that has ever reigned over us, but for the sake of
those chosen, sensitive representatives of our suffering society to whom music is equivalent to
daily bread and who seek in it a respite —
though it be only brief — from the hideous element of baseness and brutality which has us in its
grasp.*

Sergei Koussevitzky

This letter expressed Koussevitzky's negative
attitude towards the Bolsheviks so frankly that one
can only be surprised that he was not arrested at the
time. That his protest was allowed to go unpunished
may be explained on the one hand by his great popularity as an artist, and on the other by the fact that the
Bolshevik rule was then very " young," and had not

yet interfered with the liberty of the press; the bour-
geois organs, therefore, still continued their brief
existence.

In spite of his protest and rebellion Koussevitzky
did not throw in his lot with those who adopted the
methods of sabotage against the Government. For the
reasons stated in his letter, he remained at his post
as director of the State Orchestra and did not abandon
it until he went abroad.

Before the publication of Koussevitzky's protest
in the newspapers, A. Lunacharsky, the People's Commissar for Education, had offered to put him at the
head of the musical life of Russia, with full and extensive powers. Lunacharsky was very anxious to draw
Koussevitzky into the official ranks, in view of his
popularity in Russia and Europe. The Commissar un-
folded brilliant prospects before him, guaranteeing,
apart from great practical possibilities, complete freedom of action. Koussevitzky, however, declined the
proposal, on the ground that he could only work with
a government that should be recognized by the whole
of the people.

In January 1918 the Music Section of the Commissariat of National Education was established. Its duty was to superintend the musical life of Russia as a whole, and the writer of this book was appointed to take charge of it. The musicians of Moscow and Petrograd, almost without exception, actively interested themselves in the work of the section. Koussevitzky, who could not be indifferent to the fate of his country's musical culture, though occupying no official position other than that of Director of the State Orchestra, assisted in a consultative capacity in the solution of a number of very important problems affecting musical art.

Artists, scientists, musicians, and scholars were less hostile to the Bolsheviks than the rest of the community and continued to carry on their work, each in his particular sphere of activity. In comparison with their fellow-citizens they occupied a privileged position during the first year of the revolution. The Government confined itself to politics and was very cautious in its dealings with science and art. It left the workers in their fields a free hand and did not interfere in their activities.

With the discontinuance of private concerts

Koussevitzky's professional occupation as a conductor was brought almost to a standstill. The conditions in which he existed became intolerable. Just then the nationalization of industry and private property came into force, and this affected him. Everything he possessed was nationalized — houses, lands, capital, and the publishing business. Terror, hunger, cold, and want were the chief products of that year. The concerts were given in halls without heating, the audiences were frozen, and the musicians played with numbed fingers. And yet the possibility of occupying themselves with music was a great happiness. There was no bread, and art took its place. At no time and in no place have I seen people, not listening to, but devouring music with such trembling eagerness, such feeling, as in Russia during those years. . . .

In 1918 Koussevitzky conducted Tchaikovsky's *The Queen of Spades* at the Grand Opera, Moscow, then managed by a directorate, of which Koussevitzky was a member. It was a new experience for him, as he had not previously conducted in a theatre, and he gave himself up to it with great enthusiasm. On studying the score he was horrified at the supposedly

" traditional," but in reality monstrous, interpolations which he found in it. He erased them all, from the score as well as from the parts, and restored Tchaikovsky's original musical text. In his young days he had attended the rehearsals for the first production of *The Queen of Spades*, and had recollections of the fine performance obtained by Altani, the conductor — a great friend of Tchaikovsky's — and of the suggestions made to Altani at the rehearsals by the composer.

The fifth anniversary of Scriabin's death occurred in 1920. For this occasion the Music Section arranged a grand cycle of his works, extending over a whole week. All the orchestral compositions were given under Koussevitzky, and the pianoforte pieces were played by the best Russian soloists. The cycle was prefaced by a solemn gathering, at which speeches in honour of Scriabin's memory were made by poets and musicians.

It was at that time that Koussevitzky began to think of going abroad. As he could not calculate on receiving permission to leave Russia, he devised a plan of escape through Finland. This he had to abandon, as an unknown man stopped him in the street one day and warned him that his intentions were known and that the Che-ka had been trailing him for two months. This was the result of treachery on the part of a man whom he had regarded as one of his best friends. After this he resolved to proceed in legal form, and set to work to obtain the sanction of the authorities. He called on Menzhinsky at the Extraordinary Commission and asked his permission to go abroad. At first Menzhinsky refused, on the ground that if Soviet Russia lost such a conductor, it would be left without any symphonic music. Koussevitzky categorically insisted, and declared that even if he stayed in Russia, he would not appear on the platform. He said to Menzhinsky: " If I don't get permission, I shall go into the country and work on the land, so it will come to the same thing — nobody will hear a note of music from me." Menzhinsky looked at him very significantly and told him to come back for his answer in a fortnight. When Koussevitzky returned at the end of that time, to his great surprise his request was granted. After three months' worry Koussevitzky and Balmont received the first legal permits to travel.

The Koussevitzkys departed from Moscow for Reval, but were detained at the frontier, as they had no Esthonian visé. They spent a whole week in the railway carriage and then returned to Moscow for three days, obtained the visé, and got through to Reval successfully.

PART III

" It's as clear as a simple scale."

(PUSHKIN)

CHAPTER FOURTEEN

Intermezzo

(Scales)

Is that familiar to you? try to remember. you are sitting in your room in the twilight, and on the other side of the wall, or it may be below you or on the floor above — someone is playing the piano. The smothered sounds come to you as through a shroud of mist. . . . No, it's nothing in particular — only simple scales. Diatonic scales in different keys, played evenly and not too fast. Best of all, it is the not too correct tone produced by childish hands. . . . At one time it was:

"*Freischütz* played by the fingers of timid schoolgirls. . . ."

But that was in the golden age of Russian culture — in the time of Pushkin. Why, in those days we had no Conservatory and, generally speaking, no professional musicians of our own. There were only the orchestras recruited from the serfs, the aristocratic amateurs, and casual visitors from abroad. But, you know, the strange thing is that our musical culture then (not individual, but general) was not inferior to that which the succeeding period gave us.

According to Lëv Tolstoi, Natasha Rostova sang with a charm which is not possessed by the most brilliant European prima donnas of our day. In Russia the intelligentsia and the commonalty, just as did the bourgeoisie in Europe, rubbed away the enchanting patina of musical amateurism which covered the surface of the aristocratic culture of last century and which provided a foundation for the development of chamber music.

Some reminiscence of those delightful days of

old is preserved in Tchaikovsky's *The Queen of Spades,* which sparkles with the lyrical life of an age that is past. It is almost an incarnation of the memories of that life, which came later than the Pushkin period. In this sense *The Queen of Spades* is almost on the verge of a stylization. About that time everything in western Europe was corroded by professionalism. The musical traits of the past, the simple presentations of the life of the people — taken directly from it and not found in the professional efforts — were completely dissolved away, with the approval of the German musicologists. This applies particularly to the chamber-music-making at the end of last century. I am confining myself now to the development of Russian chamber music; our instrumental music and choral singing rest on entirely different foundations. Musical style (no matter where) is, of course, the result, in a literal sense, of the chamber-music art. If we bear in mind that the chamber style is the primary source from which music as a whole is fed, that instrumental and choral music alfresco is inconceivable unless it has been nourished by the chamber-music style — that intimate, lyrical atmosphere to which the elements of the cultural musical language and the style of any period owe their origin — it becomes evident that the downfall of the chamber style makes the development of great instrumental and choral music impossible, since it carries away the soil in which the latter grows; just as the decay and destruction of the family levels the foundations on which nations and empires are built. The socialist revolution is logical in breaking up the intimate family life, as the individual principle in the human race, in order to create a featureless, impersonal " people " (the proletariat), in whose name this socialist doctrine is put into operation, and applied not only to social questions, but also to the sphere of art. Thereby art, created no longer by the free will of the artist, but by the decree of political doctrinaires, is doomed to lose anything of value it possessed; it is reduced to a catastrophic impotence and is numbed up to a certain time. The more powerfully and persistently the doctrinaire effect is applied, the more impossible becomes the existence of art, and it is replaced by a pseudo-artistic product called into being by official commands, by intentions and abstract and rational constructions, which make every concession to the political demands of the moment and, in a purely artistic sense, are stamped with all the signs of creative impotence and helplessness. Since the revolution Russian music has suffered more heavily in this respect than any other art. For this the revolution is not so much to blame as the crushing effect of the Marxist dogmas, which are steadily increasing their hold on contemporary Russia and are applied not only to social and economic questions, but also to art.

Cultural Russian music (and perhaps all music) is based on the chamber-music art, which in Russia had its origin in the aristocratic culture, in the surroundings of the aristocratic life. To it we owe the whole of Glinka, but not Dargomyzhsky, his direct successor, though he wrote almost from Glinka's dictation and at first followed in the latter's footsteps. The pure culture inherited by Glinka from the eighteenth century breaks down in Dargomyzhsky, in whom we have an alloy compounded of the style of the traditional aristocratic culture obtained from Glinka and the elements of the St. Petersburg tradespeople side by side with the influence of the bourgeoisie.

That the bourgeoisie bequeathed to us not a few musical forms of artistic value is due precisely to the fact that they enjoyed a sound, solid, and plenteous existence. They left traces which played a part in the further development of the musical style; but later still, when culture was mainly in the hands of the intelligentsia, the role of the latter in music was almost entirely negative. The intelligentsia is essentially anti-musical and simply drops out of music. Aleksandr Blok once expressed it very neatly when he defined " Russia " as a musical concept, whereas " intelligentsia " was, he said, an anti-musical concept. This is cruel, but true. To admit one's intelligence (it is possible to be unconscious of it, but to admit its existence will suffice — nearly all of us are, of course, intelligent) implies that one bears the cross of the dreadful anti-musicality of his social sphere, a characteristic which every contemporary musician conquers in himself, in order to give expression to the musical element living within him. In the past there existed a genuine musical life. Its purity was a living thing, because the music grew out of life, arose in it, and was determined by it. There was no thought of "style" then; it existed of itself. Of song there is no need to speak — in our days it is the fortunate apanage of the very few. But, on the other hand, they nearly always "stylize" everything when they want to be sure of doing something good, or they risk it, and then it usually turns out to be bad. . . .

Having regard to the vulgarization existing in contemporary music, which has been transferred entirely to the streets, it is natural to dream of the restoration of musical life in the domestic circle. Why are we far more affected by music-making in comfort, amongst our friends, than in a concert hall, surrounded by an indifferent crowd? It has certainly nothing to do with moods or anything of that sort. This is a far more serious matter. The present state of things expressed itself first of all in the actual composition and performance of music. One of the most negative consequences of the transference of music to the streets is that almost every ordinary composition is written with a ready-made resonator for the concert hall, which is included in it, as an integral part of it. A certain tonal complexus, plus the concert platform. Hence the whole evil, which has turned the musical art into a vulgar trade, into a musical fair held in the interests of civilization. Hence, too, the development of a specific virtuosity having nothing in common with music. A virtuosity whose principal task seems to consist in getting out a definite number of notes in a definite unit of time, whereas genuine virtuosity seeks to display the organic tonal dynamics embodied in a musical composition.

What, then, remains in everyday life of the musical culture of the past? In our days it was only the simple diatonic scales. It is, truly, the best thing of the past; the rest of the " domestic " music played in homes would be better forgotten. It is true that in going up or down the stairs one occasionally heard Chopin, but it nearly always came from a dentist's apartments. Probably that is why Chopin badly played still gives us toothache. . . .

When we listen to scales, what do we experience? They always made me think of an hour-glass. It seemed to me that time was flowing by in a stream of sound, endless and as inevitable as eternity. It evoked a feeling of sweet melancholy, an almost lyrical emotion. I thought: " Everything is passing, we shall all die — but the scales will go on for ever."

The rhythm of those hour-glasses, which moulded our time in the diatonics of the pianoforte scales, coloured our whole outlook. It absorbed us entirely, and imperceptibly took possession of us; in it was accomplished the routine of our daily life. We were lulled to sleep in it at the end of the nineteenth century, and in the cradle of that very rhythm we awoke in the twentieth. Now it is a thing of the past; merely a reminiscence, in which the mode of existence, the family, the whole life of last century, are included. In Russia it is no more. You will say: " That's a great pity. In Europe the children still play scales." I'm afraid not. They do play, certainly, but it sounds quite different. . . .

When we had undergone our torture, and the transition from one state of existence to another had been accomplished; when, separated by the dividing line of the war and the revolution, we appeared in Europe once more — a new Europe, shaken by the historical catastrophe — we became aware in our musical consciousness of this naked, elementary sense of tone. It revealed a new state of things, which spoke of the irrevocable past, now only a memory of a tale that is told.

In contemporary Russia the old musical life was shattered to its foundations; in Latin Europe and the Germanic countries it was seriously perverted and exhausted. Possibly in England and America alone it retained its pristine purity, as an integral and vital element. I think that these countries offer a more favourable soil for the evolution of a new musical culture than anywhere else in the world. It may appear paradoxical, but England seems to me far more musical than is generally believed in Europe. For her at all events a musical renaissance, based on her forgotten traditions and revealing new perspectives, may be possible. Of course I do not assert that such is the case; I merely put it forward as a hypothesis. As regards America, there are already distinct signs that a new culture is springing up there. Though musical art in that country has hitherto been content to do little more than assimilate the musical culture of western Europe, it is possible that very soon it will manifest itself in entirely original, self-sufficing, and independent creative work. The home life of America should, in the natural course, lead her from music in the home to music on the concert platform. This is the only guarantee for the development of a genuine culture. There is always danger when the platform is kept apart from life.

In saying this I am not, of course, referring to the America which finds expression in the pursuit of gain and the struggle for existence, regardless of the means employed. I have in mind that America which is occupied in building up her spiritual culture, for whom the meaning of life is not measured by the number of monetary tokens acquired, but by the deepening of her spiritual experience. . . .

The street, the drawing-room, the concert platform, music-making in the home — such are the elements of which the contemporary musical life is composed, in which its style is originated. They are originally bound up with and react on one another. It is very difficult to discover where one sphere passes into another, but the modern musician directs the antennæ of his nervous perceptions thither and extracts nourishment for himself from all of them simultaneously.

CHAPTER FIFTEEN

Europe Once More

Although berlin was in a disastrous condition in 1920 — the aftermath of the war and the revolution — contact with Europe, even then, after a long residence in Soviet Russia, made a great impression and revived the ancient feeling that Europe was, above all things, a sort of oasis in the Asiatic continent and not a congeries of mixed nationalities; that it was the cradle of individualistic culture — the cult of personality is the essential feature of the whole of its history. The immediate result on arrival was a sense of happiness, of relief and tranquillity after the violent collectivist turmoil of Soviet Russia.

The Bolshevik's hatred of Europe is mainly based on the opposition of the individualism of Europe to the collectivism of the militant Marxist doctrine. All else is of secondary importance. Unless it has a spiritual foundation, collectivism is absolutely impossible and absurd. So far as the cultural processes of Europe were developed outside spiritual experience or in antagonism to it, to that extent individualism arose to affirm the creative manifestation of the personal principle. But directly a living spiritual experience is revealed to man, the individualistic sphere is entirely dissolved in and absorbed by that experience. Collectivism as an active principle is the sum of the personalities dissolved in man's spiritual experience. It represents the points on the spiritual plane at which men come into contact, absolutely and of their own free will, neither knowing nor suspecting one another's existence. No other collectivism exists. But the possibility of this higher spiritual collectivism (that is, spiritual reunion) depends entirely on the unconditional freedom of the individual principle. This collectivism never has been, and never will be, attained by compulsion.

The decadence of contemporary Europe, the weariness and the spiritual desolation, and the regenerating process now taking place — all this was experienced later. To perceive it one needed to study carefully and enter into the life of Europe at the time. But the first moment of contact with the West, after Soviet Russia, produced a feeling of emancipation and a delightful sensation of freedom.

When, in the spring of 1920, Koussevitzky escaped from Soviet Russia, it seemed to him that he had chanced upon another world. He completed the journey by steamer, travelling from Reval to Berlin, via Stettin. On arriving in Europe after all he had gone through in Russia, he was quite ignorant as to what awaited him. The old ties were broken; the conditions of existence had suffered a violent change. It was necessary to begin all over again. He did not know where and in what circumstances he would find a possibility of employing his powers. His stay in Berlin, in order to find out what had happened to the Russian

Music-Publishing House, was limited to two days. His nerves were exhausted by his Russian experiences, and it was out of the question to settle down and make a fresh start in a city where life was so full of difficulty and anxiety.

During the war reports had reached him in Russia that all the music-publishing businesses in Germany had been suppressed. Some of the statements made in this connexion were ridiculous; it was asserted, for instance, that the plates on which music was engraved had been melted down for bullets. It was with some anxiety, therefore, that the Koussevitzkys made their way to the Dessauerstrasse, in which the premises of the Russian Music-Publishing House were situated, expecting to find that the nest had been robbed. To their agreeable surprise, everything appeared to be in order, and even their old employé was at his post. The cash-box, however, was empty, and funds were needed to recommence operations. At the time the Koussevitzkys had no money, but later on, when he obtained engagements, a proportion of Koussevitzky's fees was allotted to the business.

The Russian Music-Publishing House had always been Stravinsky's publishers, but during the war and the revolution he had lost touch with Koussevitzky and had gone elsewhere. He now returned to his first love.

In June 1920 the Koussevitzkys went to Paris, where he at once received offers of engagements. Sergei Diagilev wanted him to conduct a ballet season, but he declined.

He was invited to Rome, to take part in concerts at the Augusteo, as conductor and double-bass soloist. He accepted the invitation and travelled to Rome in December. His appearance as a soloist was a huge success. One critic wrote: "Koussevitzky is such an artist that if, instead of his double-bass, he were given a mattress stuffed with hay, he would contrive to draw magical sounds from it."

His performance led to an engagement to give twenty concerts in Italy as a double-bass soloist. In the course of this tour a deputation waited on him with a request that he would give a recital, for which he could name his own terms, in the town in which Bottesini was born. In this town there was a genuine

SERGEI KOUSSEVITZKY
From a bust by GUIRDJAN—1920

Bottesini cult, and Koussevitzky was regarded as a worthy successor of the great contrabassist. He was, however, obliged to refuse, as he was in a hurry to get to England. His orchestral concert at the Augusteo, Rome, was broken up by a Fascist demonstration.

He was in London in January 1921 to conduct three concerts with the London Symphony Orchestra; after those he was invited to take charge of a further six. Since then he has conducted in London every season, and during that period has made two tours in Scotland with the Scottish Orchestra. His appearance in command of this body of musicians caused a sensation. The engagement with the London Symphony Orchestra has assumed an annual character.

Here he also took his own line, playing entirely new works side by side with classical music, and overcoming the conservatism of the London audiences, who are even less accustomed to new things than the French.

In the spring of 1921 Koussevitzky gave his first three concerts in Paris, at the Salle Gaveau, the programs consisting of Russian works. This was his first attempt to transfer his Russian concerts to places abroad. His design was to establish in the centre of Europe a solid and more or less durable foundation for Russian symphonic music. The circumstances surrounding the Russian colony in Paris were rather distressing. It was the period of the emigration, and the Russian émigrés, who formed the bulk of the audiences, were physically and morally in an oppressed condition. At the Koussevitzky concerts one met people who had just come through a shipwreck, so to speak. Here they found a few moments of moral refreshment, and felt themselves back in their native land, as it were. At these concerts Koussevitzky played for the first time in Paris the *Poem of Ecstasy* and *Prometheus*. The first performance was also given of Prokofiev's *Scythian Suite*, which had a great success.

Six symphony concerts were given at the Grand Opera, Paris, in the autumn of 1921, and in the following year Koussevitzky began an organized series of concerts at the Opera, four in the autumn and four in the spring. They were very brilliant affairs and recalled the surroundings of the pre-war Moscow and St. Petersburg symphony gatherings. Paris became the centre of Koussevitzky's concert activities.

At that time he commissioned Ravel to score Moussorgsky's *Pictures from an Exhibition*. This masterly piece of work was included in Koussevitzky's repertory and became very popular.

Koussevitzky's Paris seasons were highly appreciated, and, as formerly in Moscow and St. Petersburg, his concerts occupied a foremost place in the musical life of the city. For the first time in Paris they heard Russian symphonic music played as it should be played, and also made the acquaintance of a whole series of works which had not hitherto been performed there. The French press was almost unanimous in its appreciation of the concerts, pointing out the cultural work they were accomplishing and their manifest superiority over the French concert undertakings, which were very backward and responded neither to the needs of a cultured public nor to the requirements of modern musical creation and interpretation.

In addition to these concerts Koussevitzky also conducted opera. This was an entirely new role for him, and one which had hitherto interested him but little. He had three seasons of Russian opera in Spain, producing in Barcelona, for the first time with Russian artists and in the Russian language, *Boris Godu-nov*, *Prince Igor*, *The Queen of Spades*, and *The Snow Maiden*. He also gave a series of symphony concerts in Spain. The operas were so successful that these seasons are still carried on there in accordance with the Koussevitzky tradition.

Five performances took place in Lisbon, where *Boris Godunov* was produced with an orchestra completely unprepared for its task. By dint of hard work Koussevitzky obtained superb results which amply rewarded his efforts — no easy matter in Lisbon, according to his recollections.

At the time of this tour in Spain and Portugal he was invited to the Grand Opera, Paris, for the first production of *Boris Godunov* in the French language and with French artists. More than thirty performances were given to overflowing houses, and this opera became one of the most popular in the repertory. After *Boris Godunov* he staged Moussorgsky's *Khovanshchina* at the Grand Opera.

In addition to visiting England and France, Koussevitzky made frequent appearances in Berlin and Warsaw during this period.

[TRANSLATION] — My Country and my King applauded you. Don't forget that my undisciplined Philharmonic Orchestra followed your baton with heart and soul, in admiration of your art.

(*Fine Arts Club, Madrid*)

From the worst of the "second violins" of the orchestra to the eminent Maestro Koussevitzky.

(*Drawn and signed by Osés*)

France received him with open arms, and at once became his second home. The French musicians gave him a cordial welcome and adopted him as one of the family. In 1924, at the request of French artists and composers, he was made a member of the Legion of Honour for his services to French music in Russia and Europe. The occasion was celebrated by a banquet at which he was the guest of honour and which was attended by the élite of the French musical world. In the course of the proceedings facetious compositions, written by masters young and old, were performed. All the instruments, from trombone to flute, each with the graces peculiar to it, delivered their "madrigals" in his honour. In 1930 he was promoted to Officer of the Legion, a distinction which is awarded for special services, and rarely to a foreign artist.

On settling in America Koussevitzky had to devote his whole time to his work in Boston. It was impossible to get to Europe in the middle of the year. When the American concert season ended, he came over for a holiday and contrived, in spite of his fatigue, to give four concerts in Paris, in the spring of each year, for several years in succession. In 1928, however, he had to abandon them, as his work in America demanded all his energies. He was unwilling to overtax his strength, and his subsequent visits to Europe were in the nature of rest-cures.

CHAPTER SIXTEEN

A Summing-up

IN REVIEWING KOUSSEVITZKY'S CONCERT ACTIVITIES
before his departure for America, it will be seen that
they may be divided into two periods, in the first of
which he devoted himself to the propagation of western European music in Russia, and in the second to
the propagation of Russian music in western Europe.
In each instance, however, a Russian composer was
the central figure. When he returned to Europe after
the revolution, the chief places in his repertory were

occupied by Russian works, but at the same time his attitude towards Russian music had greatly changed. He had moved away from Scriabin and become the propagandist of the new musical tendencies, which then found their most convincing expression in the work of Stravinsky. The first period to which I have referred centred in Scriabin, but in the second period his place was taken by Stravinsky. How did this happen?

Scriabin was neither understood nor appreciated in Europe. He died just when his work was making some headway in the West, and his death, together with the war and the revolution, diverted what little attention Europe had begun to pay him. In the mean time the tendencies in musical art had undergone a radical alteration. New birds had appeared and they sang new songs. At Koussevitzky's Paris concerts Scriabin seemed antiquated and old-fashioned, and that frightens the snobs more than anything else. The musical essence of his creative work was incomprehensible to them, and with a shrug of the shoulders and an ironical remark they turned away. To persist in the propaganda of Scriabin meant

that Koussevitzky would be going against the spirit
of the times in western Europe, and such an attitude
towards art was never natural to him, and in the given
instance would serve no good purpose. Scriabin
dropped out of music in western Europe; history
passed him over. He seemed to be only an epigone of
Wagner, a belated Wagnerian, to which category he
was assigned. The reaction against Wagner, which set
in with the rise of impressionism, has effaced Scriabin
for years, and Heaven only knows when he will be
recalled to mind, and the genuine music that was in
that strange and aristocratically capricious art will
be plainly heard.

For Russian musicians in Russia Scriabin has
remained a star of the first magnitude, although he is
quite out of harmony with all that is taking place in
that country. There his influence has lingeringly and
obstinately persisted, but it has not been fruitful so
far as the young composers are concerned. None of
those who have come under his sway has added anything to what Scriabin himself achieved, but to this
day traces of Scriabinism, as of an unpleasant and
too protracted disease, are perceptible in the works of

the younger generation of Russian musicians now appearing in Russia.

Scriabin's place was taken by another Russian — Stravinsky. During the war and the revolution Stravinsky, who was separated from Russia and lived abroad, became the leader of nearly all the young musicians of western Europe, where the recognition denied to Scriabin was freely bestowed upon him. What Scriabin was to a whole generation of musicians in Russia during the first decade of the twentieth century, that Stravinsky was to the young European composers. After beginning on the extreme left flank of the modernists, he went through a complex evolution and appeared on the extreme right of the position. In recent years he has been the dictator of the reaction against the anarchy into which modernism degenerated. He has created a new discipline and offered in exchange for the past a new music-plastic conception, which I might describe in a few words by saying that he gave the pride of place to the formal side of art and established it as the real, fundamental substance, whilst everything else was rejected as an intrusion having no organic connexion with musical art.

The musical essence of Stravinsky's works is based on constructively objective principles of composition, and the emotional content is reduced to a minimum: consequently they lend themselves least of all to interpretation in performance. Therefore no contact has ever existed between Stravinsky and any of his interpreters. Under these conditions and quite apart from the character and quality of the performance, an almost inevitable conflict arises between the conductor and the music, because the profounder and more significant the interpretation, the more prominent the conductor's individuality becomes and the more opposed to the music he is playing. A dilemma is created, which can be solved only by the entire suppression of the conductor's personality. In handling such music he completely effaces himself and becomes, not an interpreter, but merely an impassive impersonal executant. If this does not happen and the conductor asserts himself, he thereby attains a distorted performance of the music.

Stravinsky has stated the problem of the mutual relations between composer and conductor or performer with an acuteness and a power of revelation which have never been equalled by anyone in music. For him it consists in a rigid logical and law-abiding compliance with the whole of his musical conception. His own conducting of his own compositions he does not regard as in the nature of a composer's diversion, but as a performance on a par with his music. As for the part played by any conductor who interprets his compositions, it seems to him that it is of only second-rate importance, and its value depends entirely on the ability of the conductor to subordinate himself strictly to the music and to refrain from displaying his own personality.

In his second period Koussevitzky did not confine himself to the propagation of Russian music. Unlike many others at that time, he did not become a chauvinist, but, while concentrating on Russian music, offered the hospitality of his concert platform to anything new in the music of western Europe, to which he allotted a large share of his programs. This attraction to new things has always been characteristic of Koussevitzky, and it is therefore not surprising that, on beginning his concert activities in Europe, he flung himself eagerly on anything that had appeared there

since the war and the revolution. A survey of his concerts at this period shows that he performed every
novelty of value produced during those years. He
made it possible to hear the works of the young composers and to form an impartial judgment of them.
The real critical estimate came later and of itself —
aided by the critical selection which in music always
results in a natural way. Thanks to his friendly attitude to the younger composers, his platform became
a sort of experimental laboratory for them — a laboratory with which none but Koussevitzky could or
would provide them.

Some of the works that he performed are now of
no great value. This is more or less comprehensible
when we consider the mental outlook that prevailed
during that period. Throughout the war, in the West
nothing was done in music. As a field of activity it
ceased to exist. On returning from the various fronts,
the youth of every country betook themselves eagerly
to art. These were the years of a cultural renaissance
and revival after the nightmare of the catastrophe
through which we had just come. Each of the countries that had taken part in the war reckoned up what

it had lost and what still remained whole of its spiritual and cultural treasures and like a wounded beast licked its sores. The restoration of peace was followed by a renewal and revaluation of the past. Life claimed its rights, and to all under thirty years of age it seemed that with them art was beginning to exist for the first time. They forgot history. The young people thought they were introducing a new era in art. "*De l'avant-guerre*" and "*de l'avant-garde*" were the favourite terms of criticism — were almost the only, and certainly the most fashionable, criterion. The gulf between these epithets was so vast that in looking at the skeleton of an ichthyosaurus in a museum it would have seemed quite natural to remark: "*Il est d'avant-guerre.*" Now, twelve years later, we see that in art there has really been little change; at all events, whatever was firmly rooted has not only remained, but sent its roots deeper.

To the old, something new has been added. Scriabin was succeeded by Stravinsky, a man with enormous strength of will, who with convincing authority took charge of the musical ship and steered her in another direction, diametrically the opposite of Scriabin's course. After a furious polemical and theoretical battle the position occupied by Richard Strauss was captured by Arnold Schönberg, who emerged from the cellar of the Austrian Empire to enter into the official musical life of republican Germany. On returning from the war the young German and Austrian musicians grouped themselves round Schönberg, who fed them on pap compounded of a curious mixture of anarchical æsthetics and scholastic discipline. He could not long retain the position for himself. As soon as the youngsters were weaned and had learnt something, they went off in various directions, just as they chose. From their ranks were isolated several men of strong and independent character, who occupied themselves with serious and persistent work. One such was Hindemith, who later on forsook Schönberg's ideology for Stravinsky's discipline. Schönberg in his new music has given us the most pronounced form of abstract musical composition. In his experience instrumental music has definitely lost its plastic basis and together with it any concrete vital standing. The point of support of his music is a psychological, and not a physical, corporeal gesture. As it is not grounded

laid the foundations of a new technique and a new cult of form, which took the place of the traditional schematic practice in music. That Schönberg himself became a victim of schematism, which promptly mastered him, is another matter. It was the result of his abstractness. He had no ground beneath his feet and was perforce compelled to cling to the methods created by himself, as the only reality in which he believed. His factures are so hermetically sealed that it becomes impossible to breathe; consequently performer and listener alike feel as if they were shut up in a retort. Compositions based on such a method age more rapidly than any, because they are deprived of fresh air. They maintain an atmosphere which oxidizes anything created in it. The only works which are preserved for future generations are those in which vital changes are constantly occurring and the air is kept in continual motion.

No one has occupied Debussy's place in France, and it remains vacant to this day. Temporarily — in Paris the leadership can never be permanently held by a foreigner, even if it remains with him all his life — the young musicians offered it to Stravinsky, as to a Boris Godunov. Like Boris Godunov he accepted it reluctantly, but with this difference: that he did not murder any musical tsarevich. He repaid them with interest for the honour they did him. It may be said without exaggeration that French music is entirely indebted to him for the mastering of impressionism and the new discipline. I doubt if any of those musicians who have done anything useful during the last twelve years can say that they owe nothing to him or have learnt nothing from him. Such has been his role in connexion with all the new music, not merely of France, but of Europe and America. Subsequently his influence penetrated Soviet Russia also, but there, of course, the conditions of life today are such that people have no time to think about music. . . . Stravinsky led music out of a blind alley and provided it with new perspectives and a new discipline. The future was no longer in his power, and the development of the new music was determined by the effectiveness of the available talent and the national musical peculiarities of the various countries. The affirmation of a national consciousness was the chief tendency of the young musicians of Europe after the war. These

were the years in which nationalism in music found
expression in the creation of national musical groups
— German, French, Italian, English, Spanish, Polish,
Czech, etc. All these groups seem to have taken as their
ideal, consciously or unconsciously, the Russian
" mighty band." At the time no Russian group existed, either at home or abroad.

The youth of France had the good fortune to obtain, through Koussevitzky, the possibility of the performance of their works on a large scale. In the front
rank of all the new French music given by him were
the compositions of Honegger, who at that time occupied in regard to the young French school approxi-
mately the same position as that held by Hindemith
in Germany. The latter also found in Koussevitzky a
superb interpreter of his works. Furthermore Koussevitzky did a great deal to spread the fame of Sergei
Prokofiev, who held aloof from all the tendencies
in music, whether Russian or foreign, and matured
considerably during these years. Prokofiev, Hindemith, and Honegger, the three finest post-war composers, were at the heart of the new music included
in Koussevitzky's programs, and — apart from

Stravinsky, of course — contributed the best examples of it in the second period of his concert activities. Of French composers of the older generation he paid much attention to the pillars of French modernism — Ravel, Albert Roussel, and Florent Schmitt.

In the course of these years Berlin lost its importance as the world-centre of musical culture, its place being taken by Paris. For various reasons the French musicians have not known how to profit by the situation, but a return to the musical hierarchy which existed at the end of the nineteenth century is, in the present circumstances, quite impossible.

CHAPTER SEVENTEEN

America

In 1924 KOUSSEVITZKY WAS INVITED TO TAKE CHARGE of the Boston Symphony Orchestra. He accepted the invitation and arrived at Boston in the autumn of that year. He found the conditions and circumstances quite different from those to which he had been accustomed in Russia and Europe. As we have already seen, his work during his first, or Russian, period and his second, or European, period was to a large extent controlled by his actual environment and the musical traditions prevailing, and he orientated himself accordingly. In America, however, art was not fettered by tradition, and he therefore had a free hand and was able to take an independent line; he had not to adapt himself to previously existing conditions, but could shape his surroundings to his will. In this we have the distinguishing feature of the third period of his career as a conductor. It needed all his experience as a conductor and his ripe mastery to enable him to act thus in an entirely new country and in circumstances which prevented him from assuming the initiative to which he was habituated — in the circumstances of an artist who had been summoned to guide the destinies of a great social and musical organization which had existed before he came. The brilliant results and the unqualified triumph attending his efforts are due to the clear-cut, confident, and decisive attitude which he at once assumed and which excluded the possibility of any aimlessness, unevenness, or vacillation.

The Boston Symphony Orchestra, founded in 1881, already had a glorious past. From 1900 to 1914, when it reached the highest point of its develop-

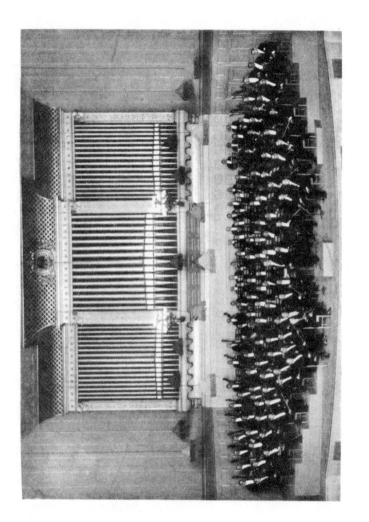

THE BOSTON SYMPHONY ORCHESTRA

ment, it was one of the finest orchestras in the world, for which position it was indebted to three famous men — Wilhelm Gericke, Arthur Nikisch, and Karl Muck, who brought it to the pitch of perfection it eventually attained. In the economical and political conditions resulting from the war it suffered some decline. Its activities were curtailed, although its ranks still included some superb musicians and it worked under serious conductors. Its numbers were reduced by the defection of players who were attracted to the great centres — New York, Philadelphia, and Chicago. At the time of Koussevitzky's invitation the Boston Symphony Orchestra, in addition to the cadre of old members who had worked with it for thirty or forty years and were not equal to modern requirements, was cumbered with a certain number of players of an average quality, recruited during the war. The first-class musicians who still remained with it were swallowed up in the general mass. It was with such a body that Koussevitzky had to begin his work here. He found an abominable routine and a lack of discipline. The concerts had lost their former prestige, and subscriptions had almost ceased. In such a state of things he had either to refuse the conductorship or to reorganize the orchestra from top to bottom. He decided to remain. Difficulties did not frighten him, and with the energy natural to him he turned up his sleeves and set to work. The first steps to be taken were clearly indicated — there must be sweeping changes, since it was impossible to carry on with the forces at his disposal. His chief difficulty was the veterans who fell below the level of the new conductor's high standard. To get rid of these men was very difficult; from a humanitarian point of view it is self-evident that it is impossible to turn adrift people who have spent their whole lives in some particular form of employment; and art, in so doing, is cruel and merciless. But from an artistic standpoint the very first thing to be done is to pension them off and replace them by new musicians worthy of the name. When Koussevitzky began to take steps in this direction, the veterans raised a regular storm about his ears. Each of them had a family and friends, influence, and connexions in the city as well. Koussevitzky approached the question boldly: he submitted a scheme of reorganization to the trustees of the orchestra, based on radical changes in its composition. After some hesitation the trustees gave him a free hand.

Koussevitzky soon improved the discipline and brought it to an ideal condition. The following season thirty-six excellent musicians were added to the personnel of the orchestra. He continued to change its composition, renewing it to a considerable extent and supplementing it with fresh forces. Now it consists entirely of young people — the captain has a young crew and with all sail set is steering his ship towards new shores.

The interest in the concerts at once began to revive; so much so that in the second season, at Boston, New York, and all the cities in which the orchestra usually appears, the whole of the subscribers returned and subscriptions were received long before the concerts commenced. Finding it inadvisable to visit some of the smaller towns, Koussevitzky omitted them from his tours, and in their stead insisted on increasing the number of concerts in the university centres of New England; he also announced a new subscription series in Boston itself. All this was done, with profitable results.

Having solved the administrative problem in this brilliant fashion, he turned his attention to the artistic side of the business and was equally successful there. Before his arrival the programs had been built up without system, impersonal, and casual; they now acquired a freshness and were drawn up logically and with a sense of proportion and harmoniousness. And whereas it had been the custom to engage soloists for the performance of hackneyed pieces of which everyone was weary, he employed them only when they were necessary for the production of works.

In the six years spent with the Boston Orchestra Koussevitzky not only has accomplished the task he undertook, but has raised the orchestra to a position higher than it had previously attained at any time. Now, on its fiftieth anniversary, it is in the plenitude of its powers and, according to general and unquestioned opinion, is the finest body of musicians in the world. For Boston it has become an object of continual pride, and one of the greatest treasures of a cultured city. Every member of the orchestra occupies an honoured and flattering position in the country, and its tours are always attended with enormous success.

For the hundredth anniversary of Beethoven's death Koussevitzky organized, in 1927, a Beethoven festival, at which all the symphonies and the last quartets were performed. The surroundings in which it took place made Boston the centre of the Beethoven celebrations in America, just as Vienna was in Europe.

Summing up Koussévitzky's work in America for the last six years, we come to the conclusion that the third period of his activities as a conductor has been an international one. Whereas, as we have already shown, he devoted his first period principally to the propagation of European music in Russia, and his second pre-eminently to the propagation of Russian music in Europe, his third period has been essentially international and has not been limited to any particular tendency. He has not shown a preference for any one composer nor fostered one school at the expense of another. In a word, he cannot be reproached with partiality or with the inculcation of his personal tastes. He has been extremely objective and eclectic. His artistic capital has comprised the old and new music of all lands. His repertory is based on the German classics — Bach, Handel, Haydn, Mozart,

Beethoven, Schubert, Schumann, and Brahms. He introduced Brahms to Boston, where he had been respected, but very little played. Koussevitzky made him a very popular composer. In the season of 1930 he arranged a Brahms festival, which lasted six days.

Koussevitzky's repertory is enormous. During his first two years in America he gave fifty-two orchestral programs without repeating a single work. The possession of such a repertory gives him an exceptional position among contemporary conductors, owing to his excellent knowledge of three schools — the Russian, the German (acquired during his residence in that country), and the French (the result of his long-existing attachment to and love for French culture).

Of course he continued to be, as he had always been, a faithful friend to new music, and from the very beginning of his work in America he made a point of supporting every American composer of talent. He immediately began to seek out anything of value that had been created in the sphere of American music and to include it in his concert programs. At the same time he performed American music at his

Paris concerts and thereby spread a knowledge of it in a city which had hitherto been ignorant of its existence. This attitude towards them was naturally very helpful and stimulated the creative powers of the young composers, who found in him a moral and artistic stay and an ideal interpreter of their intentions.

America did not remain in debt to Koussevitzky. Here he was very quickly appreciated and rewarded according to his merits — his talents as an artist, his energy as an organizer, and his qualities as a social and musical worker being duly valued. In recognition of his services to the musical culture of the country Brown University, Providence, conferred on him the degree of doctor "*honoris causa*" in 1926, and in 1929 the distinction of LL.D. was awarded him by Harvard University. This was one of the highest honours America could offer him.

In his repertory and in the general character of his work Koussevitzky stands between two generations of conductors, On the one hand he is connected with the traditionalists, whose interpretation of classical music he once accepted; on the other he represents a stage on the road which led to the new, modernist school. He was almost the first to propagate new music, and in so doing he prepared the way for the younger generation of conductors, who follow in his footsteps and encounter no obstacles. Indeed, at the present time a conductor who is possessed of any culture finds himself obliged continually to perform new works, in compliance with the demands of the press and the public.

In comparing Koussevitzky with contemporary workers in the field of art, I am reminded of S. P. Diagilev. Though differing essentially in character, culture, and tastes, they have something in common in the nature of their work. The one propagated the Russian ballet in Europe, the other established Russian symphonic music in Europe and America. Both contributed largely to the dissemination of Russian art beyond the bounds of Russia. Like Diagilev, Koussevitzky does not content himself merely with performing any new music of value; he stimulates the creative process by commissioning new works from composers and at the same time leaving them a free hand. The changing fortunes of many of the artistic aspirations and the rapid exhaustion of the attractions which led to various quests during the existence of the Diagilev ballet are explained by the headlong tempo of Diagilev, who was always unwearying and persistent in the search for some new thing. But for Diagilev's ardent temperament in matters concerning art, and his passionate yearning for novelty, the existence of the various tendencies would have dragged on indefinitely, whereas it proceeded at lightning speed. In this respect Koussevitzky is at one with Diagilev. His intense activity in regard to new music leads to a more rapid development of the creative process in the young composers whose music he plays, as he will not allow them to mark time; he demands a continuous forward movement and the maximum exertion of their powers. In this way he promotes among them a constant re-appraisement of their work, as a result of which everything that falls below the general level is rejected and eventually excluded from the sphere of his activities, and only that which has a genuine and incontestable value is retained. As for the artistic temperature of this music, its objective estimate will be established by time alone.

In writing this biography I have not been content

merely to discuss the facts of Koussevitzky's life and the materials referring to his activities which I had at my disposal, but have attempted at the same time a general outline of the musical art of the first quarter of this century and of the present day. I have taken a sort of bird's-eye view of the subject and have therefore intentionally confined myself to generalities and have not dwelt on details.

As the outcome of the prevailing historical, social, and political conditions, America has lately been promoted to the leading position in respect of the intensive process of musical culture developing there. I do not refer to the creative work accomplished by her, but to the economic side of the musical art, in regard to which she has become the leading market of the musical world. This has led to a correlation of forces which may seem to be fraught with serious consequences for Europe. The symptoms are sufficiently important to warrant our paying some attention to what is going on. Mainly owing to economic causes, America has become the centre of attraction for the finest musicians of western Europe. America guarantees them the most favourable material conditions, and consequently the best executant talent of the musical world is at her disposal. But America attracts the interpretative element only and not the creative one — in the first place because the former alone has up to the present been adopted there, and secondly because it is essentially more " international " than the latter, which is far more firmly attached to its cultural and national roots than the artistic interpreter.

What, then, is happening in America? Music there has come to be largely an object of luxury. It is not a natural product of the soil, but has been artificially engrafted upon the material prosperity of the country. To this day America owes her musical culture almost entirely to the forces of Europe, with the help of those musicians who, attracted at first by material gain, have gradually become "culture-carriers." European musicians who have long worked in America and have been absorbed in the building up of its culture become, imperceptibly to themselves, Americanized. By degrees they lose the link with the culture in which they were trained, and are durably bound up with the one in course of creation there.

They rightly belong to America — they constitute the first layers of her musical and artistic agglomeration, whilst those who do not form part of this agglomeration, who have preserved a living connexion with their national cultural bases, are the ferments, the yeast, without which the musical dough will not rise. Beyond question America has the finest materials with which to develop a musical culture — the best orchestras in the world, libraries, laboratories, etc. Under such conditions she is naturally attracted by the idea of becoming the centre of the world's music, but the value of an artistic culture depends, of course, not on material welfare, but on a number of other things. Material prosperity may play a great part in its evolution, but cannot be the main factor in its creation.

The supreme value of a country's musical culture consists, not in its concert and teaching activities, but in the music which is directly created in that country. Failing the latter, its musical culture, even though it has brilliant resources at its command, is merely superficial. It is an object of luxury for the few and does not become a factor in the development of a general culture, a spiritual treasure of the whole nation.

The fundamental task of music in America, its most important problem, is the stimulation of creative work. This question should be its chief concern, and all the rest of America's musical life should be carried on with reference to it. Given this, in view of the foundation which is already laid and the vast accumulation of musical and artistic resources ready to hand, it should be possible to build up a new and independent creative musical art. Of course, even under conditions most favourable to the erection of an ideal edifice on the musical and artistic substructure already provided, the solution of the problem depends first and foremost on the availability of creative powers and on their value. But the manifestation of these powers — so far as they exist or even merely appear to exist — is largely conditioned by the circumstances in which they are compelled to operate. The problem of an American school of composers, a national school, is very complex. It seems to me to be entirely different from those with which western Europe was faced, and I regard it from another aspect. The adaptation of the methods of western Europe to musical creation in America is, I think, a narrowing of the American problem, a development on the line of least resistance, based on a repetition of the stages through which Europe has already passed or is now passing. Whereas the contemporary state of western European music is due to a special series of factors, for her decisive, the conditions prevailing in America are of quite another order, and there is no need for her to depend on the musical happenings in present-day Europe.

At the moment I cannot devote myself to a survey of this question in all its complexity. Nevertheless, I permit myself to set forth here a few propositions which seem to me fundamental.

In the ideological sphere a peculiarity of American music, which distinguishes it from the music of western Europe, is the absence of any tragic meaning, of tragic pathos, the result being that it lacks a metaphysical substratum. On the other hand, it thereby obtains in compensation that special kind of optimism which appears to be an attribute of the American artistic temperament. Permeated with the spirit of optimism, musical creation here may rest on a simplified, but, on the other hand, a healthily emotional, foundation, which of itself is supremely valuable and very essential for the future. It may happen that an individual artist will be " pessimistic." But then he will prove to be in conflict with the general historic and cultural development of America, which has no pessimism in its make-up. In relation to American culture such an artist will be a " foreign body," an exception. In Europe we see just the opposite: contemporary art as a whole is imbued with pessimism. Creative optimism there is an individual phenomenon, an exception to the general spirit. . . .

In the matter of serious musical endeavour there seems to me to be a good deal of vacillation. American composers do not so much create their own technical means of expression as make use of the achievements of western Europe, adapting them to their own ends, regardless of the fact that they may be of a popular nature and not of the highest order. But in respect of basic musical material American music does contain some exceptionally valuable and entirely independent examples, which are an acquisition to American history and American culture.

The hesitation in regard to form is particularly evident in the American composers' treatment of folk-lore, to which they are so strongly attracted. Not because folk-lore is obsolete — essentially it is not — but because in their hands it becomes a fortuitous and not an organic entity, chosen in accordance with the dictates of taste. Knowing that it played a very serious part in the creative music of various European countries, some American composers use folk-lore arbitrarily in their compositions, selecting it at random from one or other of the native American races, though they have no real organic need of it and are equally indifferent as to whether or not a living bond exists between themselves and it.

Fundamentally the American school of composition is cosmopolitan. This is the key to the solution of its problem in regard to musical creation. Whereas in western Europe, no matter in what country, creative music has accomplished and is still accomplishing its destiny by abandoning national in favour of universal art, America's problem consists in the vanquishing of her cosmopolitanism, which in America is comparable to nationalism in Europe, and the acquisition of a new, organic, super-national artistic culture. Creative practice in American music at the present time finds expression in two directions: either it masters cosmopolitanism, in which case the composers reveal the outlines of a new culture, vague as yet; or it fails to do so, and then their racial, cultural, and national peculiarities overcome them and send them back to the sources to which they are individually indebted for their appearance on the scene. On the composers included in the first category depends the whole future of the musical art of the country; they are the real creators, whereas the others are only the epigones of an experiment which has had its day in western Europe.

CHAPTER EIGHTEEN

Technique and Interpretation

FROM THE OUTSET OF HIS CAREER AS A CONDUCTOR, Koussevitzky had to deal with a new acoustic problem in relation to the orchestra. He was always seeking a new sonority, which would respond to the feelings of the contemporary listener and would not be a repetition of the traditional routinism, disguised as a pseudo-restoration of the past. He set the nerves tingling and introduced an animation and a vital force which were characteristic of him from the very first.

He imbibed sonorousness as such and devoted the whole strength of his unbridled musical temperament to the creation of tonal orgies. A passionate lover of tone, he blasted up the musical element and, intoxicated beyond measure by it, played arbitrarily and capriciously with his power as its tamer, now subjugating it, now delving once more in the abysses of the musical chaos. . . .

Thus the first impulses of youth found an outlet. In those years whatever he performed was for him only an occasion for the capricious play of his temperament with the musical element. A performance was converted into a passionate duel, in which he was nearly always the victor; but there were times when he came away from a concert as dishevelled as if he had just emerged from a cage of lions who had suddenly refused to obey their tamer and had flung themselves upon him as though he were an enemy. The audience who witnessed these thrilling spectacles and rewarded him with a storm of applause had no suspicion of the serious danger to which he was exposed, as they were quite unaware that the musical element is a far more terrible beast than the lion or the tiger.

Later on he occupied himself in working out the various kinds of sonorities revealed in the compositions of the different composers and periods which he performed. In this sphere he attained a high state of perfection and a keen insight into the subject. To this practice he owes his eclecticism. The eclecticism of the performer differs from that of the creator. The creative artist, having no style of his own, creates his manner by combining a number of styles already in being. But the eclecticism of the performer is a skilful reincarnation of himself in the various existing styles, with an equally active and vital attitude towards each of them. Lacking this eclecticism he is restricted to one school or even to a single composer. The more points of application for his technique a conductor finds, the wider his range and the richer his possibilities, the more eclectic he becomes. Those who assert that there can be no interpretation apart from eclecticism are perfectly correct.

For the performer eclecticism is also one of the chief requisites to the attainment of universalism, whereas universalism in creative work is achieved without the assistance of eclecticism of any kind.

Koussevitzky is a typical eclectic conductor. He plays music belonging to entirely different schools and tendencies with equal feeling and enthusiasm and without experiencing any sense of an inward struggle.

The sonority of Koussevitzky's orchestra is based on the tone of the strings; hence its remarkable singing quality, which predominates over everything else. The distinguishing feature of his technique is that he always secures a clarified leading of the voices no matter what he plays. The contrary method is to superimpose the melody on the rest of the orchestral sonority, which does not give it a singing character. He very rarely employs the latter method, but nearly always aims at making the whole instrumental facture of the work he is performing lyrical. Thanks to this quality of his technique, he often produces the impression (especially in new music) of an artificial melos in compositions entirely deprived of melody, and thereby temporarily endows them with the life which is really lacking in them.

The string tone to which I have referred appears to be the result of Koussevitzky's experience as a double-bass player, which gave him an exceptional knowledge of the stringed instruments. To his mind they supply the key to orchestral colouring. The basing of the orchestral sonority on string tone explains, I think, Koussevitzky's propensity for slow tempos — a propensity which he always had and which is very characteristic of him. By using them he opens out the bar-lines, so to speak, and lets the " air " in, with the object of allowing everything in the score to come through, thereby making sure that it reaches the listener. To a certain extent we find signs of this in his attitude to tempo, which for him has a relative and not an absolute significance. His technique of tempo is based on the fact that he determines it, not from the fundamental metrical structure of a composition, but from the secondary parts, which he finds in the accompaniment, or even in the harmonic figuration. As a rule he does not conduct a work according to its metre. He conducts the music, but does not beat time, as he considers it unnecessary and relies on the orchestra's sense of metre. His impression is that the emotional strain experienced by the conductor is never so great as in those moments when he folds his

SERGEI KOUSSEVITZKY
From a canvas by PETROFF-VODKIN — 1925

arms and leaves the orchestra to itself. This method
is very typical of him and he often employs it. In his
technique it belongs to the category of magical gestures. Instead of his hands he makes use of his eyes
to hypnotize the orchestra and produces a greater
effect with them than with the movements of his hands.
Nikisch, who played in Wagner's orchestra as a young
man, remembers that at certain moments of intense
musical exaltation Wagner all but ceased to conduct.
He raised his hands and led the musicians with his
whole being, no longer beating time, thereby creating
an unusually powerful impression. In Koussevitzky's
technique the traditional beat associated with the
rationalistic methods of conducting has in general no
significance. The position of the hands in the air, and
the character of the beat, are to him equivalent to the
virtuoso's touch, and also serve to maintain the bal-
ance of tone. For him gesture has a dramatic, or even
a plastic, meaning. When on the platform, it is natural for him to feel almost like an actor playing a dramatic part. This feeling was with him in his young
days and he has never lost it. The gestures he uses in
conducting seem to him almost the counterpart of the

plastic art in dramatic acting. Plastic gesticulation applied to a musical phrase enables him to get more out of it than he could obtain by beating time in the usual way.

Such are the main features of Koussevitzky's technique. As for the rehearsals preparatory to the concerts, they are carried on in a very rationalistic style and in full accordance with tradition. Koussevitzky is not an improvisator and does not rely on inspiration to bless his appearances on the platform. He regards a concert as a sort of revised version of the results obtained at the rehearsals. The fruits of inspiration, if they manifest themselves, are only an agreeable addition to all the rest. He requires the musicians to give of their best at rehearsals, as he considers that by so doing their labours will be rewarded, even though the concert performance may not be above the average. At the concert itself Koussevitzky undergoes a change. He becomes, to use his own expression, "possessed" by the musical sounds, which evoke in him something akin to a mediumistic condition. Whatever his state of weariness or enervation at another time, directly the music begins, all this vanishes in an instant and he feels himself a new and vigorous man, clad in the panoply of his resources.

The problem of interpretation is one in which Koussevitzky is intensely interested — to him the conductor's art is an interpretative art *par excellence.* He is not satisfied with a bare and impersonal reproduction of the musical text without any assistance from his intellect; he gives in his performance a free interpretation of the work he is playing, after filtering it through his perceptions and feelings. But there are two types of performance, two methods of interpretation. In the one the performer gets inside a composition, removes the layers with which it has become encrusted during its existence, and polishes up the resonance. The other method leads the performer away from the composition and towards himself. The work he is playing serves him merely as an excuse to talk about himself, to tell us of the personal experiences evoked by contact with it. The use of both methods is natural to Koussevitzky and it is difficult to say which he prefers. With him the choice is not deliberately made, but is rather the outcome of the feelings evoked in him by the composition he is performing.

Indeed, generally speaking, the types of interpretation to which I have referred exist nearly always and to a large extent subconsciously and not as the result of cold reasoning. The less important a work is, the more it becomes nothing but material for the conductor. He absorbs it, dissolves it in his musical consciousness, treats it in his own way, and makes the most he can of it. The tonal possibilities of important compositions require much time and practical experience for their realization, and the sonorities hidden in them have to be polished up and brought out into the daylight. Only after this preliminary work has been accomplished — often a matter of years — does the absolute artistic perspective, the real musical value, of a given composition become clear; only then do we obtain in its interpretation a tonal, formal, and ideological equilibrium.

Before a musical work of supreme importance is presented to its hearers in its true light, it goes through three historical stages. In the first it exists only as raw tonal material. In the second stage it is overgrown with the accretions left on it by the various performers through whose hands it has passed, and retains traces

of the different interpretations and periods. In the
third stage all this is rubbed away and obliterated,
and the interpreter instinctively reverts to the pure
form of the given work, striving to recover it as it
was at first, save that the crudities which it then contained are now toned down and a highly polished version is presented to us.

Such is the historical canvas of a musical chef-
d'œuvre from the moment of its conception to the
moment of its canonization, and such are the fundamental ways and means of musical interpretation.
Apparently no others exist. Not a few decades passed
before the treasures contained in Beethoven's symphonies were fully revealed to the world.

There can be no doubt that Wagner, Berlioz, and
Bülow gave wonderful performances of Beethoven.
But in their time Beethoven's symphonies were passing through their second stage and were commented
upon in all kinds of ways. Undoubtedly Wagner, Berlioz, and Bülow expressed themselves more than
Beethoven in performing his symphonies. I think we
may conclude that he is better and more faithfully
expounded nowadays; not because the contemporary

conductors are superior to these three men, but in virtue of the historical conditions and perspective.

In regard to the composer's attitude towards the performance of his works, if he is a really good artist, he cares only for the crude sonority in which they first saw the light. The second, interpretative stage, in which all the possible interpretations of them come to maturity, he rejects more or less decisively, considering them to be disfigurements; whilst of his relation to the third stage nothing is known, since no composer has heard his compositions played after a lapse of several epochs.

Of course, I do not claim that my theory of interpretation is not open to argument, but it seems to me most convincing, and I put it forward as a hypothesis containing a possible reconciliation and solution of the problem, both for the supporters of interpretation in music and for those who repudiate it.

himself; that if he were given the opportunity, he would astonish the world. As a matter of fact that is so; any musician can conduct, but he will do it badly, since to do it well is an art that cannot be taught. For this he must be born into the world with something that others do not possess. The public understands nothing about orchestral conducting, as it has absolutely no standard by which to form an opinion on the subject, but it is by no means indifferent to the personality of the conductor, whose physical appearance has a great deal to do with its approval or disapproval of him. In the early days of their acquaintance the public esti- mate of him is based almost entirely on this physical sympathy or antipathy. If no physiological contact is established, the most brilliant musical qualifications will fail to accomplish their purpose, and between the public and the conductor there will exist a yawning gulf of coldness and tediousness. . . . The conduc- tor's art is created by an indissoluble combination of qualities, especially the musical, psychological, and physical. His technique is the reciprocal action of these three categories — the three dimensions of his art, so to speak. The professional side of the business

—the technical skill, experience, practice, and all the rest of it—is of secondary importance.

This means, of course, that we are far more ready to forgive a conductor for a technical blunder in the performance of a symphony (a blunder which, by the way, is rarely noticed by any save himself and the specialists) than for his manners, which will irritate instead of captivating us.

In the conductor's art the personal charm peculiar to the artist plays a very important role, and the public is drawn into the magic circle of the musical act only when the magician's wand is in the hands of a man whose very personality has a significance, apart altogether from the professional side of his performance.

The conductor thus becomes the hero of the musical crowd. By analogy with the hero of tragedy he should be able to alter his impersonation to accord with the period, character, and style of the music he is performing. The qualities of his technique will also display themselves in this flexibility and in the convincingness of his personification. The conductor's role differs from that of the hero on the stage, inasmuch as it is complicated by the fact that the former is the sole optical focus; upon him are concentrated and crystallized the complex, multiform will and psychology of the musicians forming the body of the orchestra. The will and the psychology of each individual member are paralysed by the conductor and converted into a single will and a collective psychology, and through him alone they find expression. Having absorbed them, he has to bring them into living accord with himself, and only when this current is closed does the musical act begin. Such is the basic material from which the musical art is created.

The tone material is supplied by the players themselves and undergoes some form of elaboration by the conductor, but the stuff of which his art is made has less to do with the musical material than with the human will and psychology. Therefore the same orchestra will sound quite differently under different conductors. The result of practice and experience is that a moment suffices to establish contact by the replacement of the collective musical consciousness of the orchestra by the individual musical consciousness of the conductor. The resistance of the material plays the same part here as in any other art. Here it is the will and psychology of living men, and in overcoming its resistance the art of the conductor is created, just as the composer, the painter, the poet, the sculptor, create their arts by mastering the refractory materials with which they work.

Koussevitzky responds fully to those fundamental demands made by his art. A born conductor, he has found in it the normal and most complete expression of himself. It is possible to disagree with him and to impugn this or the other feature of his interpretation, but it is impossible to deny that conducting is a part of himself, since it is the organic manifestation of his musical entity. His technique (including his interpretation) is composed of a number of the factors to which I have referred — it is the result of a prolonged evolutionary process and of a mixture of heterogeneous elements. It is most characteristic of him that he belongs to the category of modernist conductors and not to the class of traditional conductors. He is an exponent of the new technique of conducting, which came into being with the new music of the twentieth century, and seems to carry on the Nikisch line. There is nothing of traditional formalism in his art. The sonority of his orchestra, his expression, the metrical and rhythmical relations established by him, the dynamic, the feeling for a cultivation of nuance, all these elements in his technique and interpretation are certainly the specific outcome of the musical culture which originated in the modernist period and have nothing in common with anything previously existing in this sphere. The evolution accomplished by him from complexity to simplicity — from the subtly capricious expression characteristic of the beginning of his career to the clear-cut, simple lines for which he has striven in recent years — his transition from nervous excitement and broken rhythms to evenness of movement, to metrical and rhythmical equilibrium — all this together does not imply a return to the traditional and formal canon of conducting which once prevailed. In everything he does and whatever the means he employs, Koussevitzky is invariably a modernist. In his latest attainments in this direction there are traces of classicism, but it is a classicism of a special kind, expressed in the crystallization of the style of the modernist musical period. To the extent to which that period may be regarded as closed, to that extent its style has become crystallized, the process being assisted by the simplification and generalization of the style. Just as we may consider Debussy's music classical in comparison with what it seemed to be twenty-five years ago, so the technique and interpretation resulting from Koussevitzky's evolution are classical when compared with their predecessors at the beginning of his career. In his conducting he sums up the achievements of his life, which embraces the modernist period in its entirety. His keenly subjective, arbitrary, and capricious artistic temperament at first found expression in audacity and innovation, but eventually wisdom taught him sobriety and he attained the equilibrium of a ripe mastery. His very mastery, however, has been nourished on the products of his own period and of no other; he has never avoided it nor hidden himself from it, but has always taken from it everything he needed. That is why the distinguishing traits of his technique and interpretation are organically connected with his own times. He has opened up his path to the end, but it may be that still greater perfection lies ahead of him, since art knows no limits; I think that for him, however, it is possible only in the same direction. It can hardly be imagined that his future activities will undergo a sudden and decisive change, a rupture with the culture with which he has hitherto been associated, and that he will engage in new and completely unexpected quests following other roads than those which modernism has trodden. Still, one never knows what may happen and this may be possible, but we will form no conjectures on the subject.

Whatever the future may hold for Koussevitzky, he has done great things in the past and has devoted a quarter of a century to their accomplishment. His mastery is complete and mature, he has penetrated the depths of the greatest musical creations, thereby increasing his interpretative powers, and the experience he has acquired is rich and varied. Whatever he may ultimately achieve, we cannot doubt that it will always be an important and valuable contribution to the conductor's art, or that in the history of music his name will be among those who have actively and assiduously co-operated in the development of musical culture during the present century.

I think the most characteristic thing about Koussevitzky is that he is a Russian conductor. No Russian school of orchestral conducting seems to have existed at any time. There have been men of high standing, but they have been isolated figures, having no connexion with one another and nothing in common save the general features peculiar to the Russian conductor's art and to the character and style of Russian interpretation. That there is no school of conductors linked together by a great inherited cultural tradition is probably due to the simple fact that Russian music itself is a very young art. It must not be forgotten that it is only a century old, and that its symphonic music is younger still.

It may now be confidently asserted that, side by side with the Italian and German schools, we now have a Russian school of performance and interpretation. It is time to recognize and admit that the culture and technique of this school are completely emancipated and no longer depend on the Germans or the Italians, to whom we Russians, creators and performers, have in the past been greatly indebted. Our school has come into existence as an independent and equally valuable artistic form. In the conductor's art it finds its completest expression in the person of Koussevitzky. First of all, he is a Russian conductor, and the best of them, since their ranks contain no one who can even be compared with him. He is the first Russian conductor to develop the interpretative methods and the culture of orchestral performance beyond the strictly national boundaries within which his predecessors confined themselves. Here we see the immediate and organic dependence existing between musical performance and musical creation in any period or country. The creative music of Russia, which in the first era of its history was a " provincial " art in relation to western Europe, long ago freed itself from that provincialism, and in so doing also liberated the performer's art. Finding its self-determination in folk-music and having undergone a rapid evolution, it not only rose to the level of universal music, but in our time has become the leader of the musical art of the world. The executive art, following in its footsteps, has also arrived at maturity and has progressed from the national to the universal plane.

The creative music of contemporary Europe ad-

SERGEI KOUSSEVITZKY
Photograph by GARO

mits the part played by Russian music and confirms it by the close attention it pays to the Russian experience of the past and by its persistent adaptation to Russian experience of today.

In the last twenty-five years we have witnessed the wide propagation of symphonic music. Now we find in the big cities nearly everywhere orchestras playing serious music, and their number is constantly increasing. Simultaneously there is a growth in the army of music-lovers, but they are far outnumbered by the lovers of spectacle, and I am not sure whether musical art is becoming more necessary and important in the life of today than it was in the past, in spite of the enormously extended area it covers. For me this remains an open question.

The art of the twentieth century started out under the banner of idealism and idealistic aspirations. The beginning of the century appeared to be an era of lofty idealism, in the light of which its predecessor was considered to be a rationalistic and materialistic age — the age of reason. We now see that it was not really so. To us who are living in the atmosphere of super-materialism, with which not only contemporary art but contemporary culture as a whole is surrounded, the people of the nineteenth century appear to have been incomparable dreamers, idealists, and visionaries.

The spirit of music in mankind does not increase. At best it exists now to the same extent as hitherto, with this difference: that, whereas it was formerly the possession of eminent individuals, in whom it was concentrated with unusual power, today it is dissipated among the multitude. . . . But the presence of even a small particle of it is sufficient to discriminate the sheep from the goats, since " many are called, but few are chosen." To those who are marked by the spirit of music power is given to " make well-up the springs " and " move the hearts of men." . . .

Music breaks through the increasing clatter of modern civilization with a voice that is barely audible. In the hurly-burly with which we are surrounded, what is music now? Who needs it?

We know that poetry has departed from us and has almost ceased to exist. Will the musician share the poet's fate?

" What will become of our world if music forsakes us? " — this question was asked by Gogol nearly a hundred years ago. What would he say now?

All these problems are very disturbing and significant, but they transgress the limits of my subject, and so I leave the reader to solve them, assuming that, whatever the fate of art now and in the future, the path of the true artist will always lead in the final reckoning to one end: in the words of the poet, he is

Au fond de l'Inconnu pour
trouver du Nouveau! . . .

By Way of Conclusion

. . . WHAT A THEATRE! IT'S WORTH DESCRIBING. You look at the stage — and see nothing, because there are tallow candles in front of your nose and they sear your eyeballs. You look behind you — and see nothing, because it's dark. You look to the right — and see nothing, because there's nothing there. You look to the left — and see the chief of police in a box. The orchestra consists of four clarinets, two double-basses, and one violin, which the bandmaster scrapes. A remarkable thing about this bandmaster is that he's deaf, and when it's time to begin or leave off, the first clarinet tugs his coat-tails, and a double-bass beats time on his shoulder with his bow. Once, out of personal spite, he hit the bandmaster so hard that the latter turned round and was about to let fly at him with the fiddle, but at that moment the clarinet twitched the bandmaster's coat-tails and he fell backwards on to the drum and went through the skin. He picked himself up in a hurry and wanted to continue the fight, but, oh horror! instead of his military head-piece the drum was smacked on his head. The house was in a frenzy of delight, the curtain was lowered, and the orchestra was obliged to depart to the police station. While the fun was on, I was wondering what was going to happen.

Of course you think, Sergei Alexandrovitch, that I've written this in a sort of musical delirium and you're astonished. No, my dear friend. It's taken from a letter of Lermontov's to his friend Lopukhin. Doesn't it seem to you that it might have come out of Hoffmann, whom we both love? Why, it might have been recorded somewhere in the memoirs of the mad but pathetic kapellmeister Kreisler, whom I always regarded from my childish years as the ideal type of

a musician. May this page from the Russian Kreis-
leriana remind you of our native land! There ought
to have been something of the kind in the Vyshny
Volochek theatre, in which you first made music as a
small boy. I suppose you weren't one of those contra-
bassists who beat time with his bow on the shoulder
of a deaf old bandmaster? Perhaps something similar
flashes across your mind when you stand before the
huge, ideally organized and disciplined musical nest
of the Boston Symphony Orchestra and, listening to
the roll-call, notice how each of the birds in the nest
with keen attention watches and obeys a movement
of your hands. That shows how far you have travelled.
The pathos of distance, as Nietzsche says. It must be a
great satisfaction to you to feel that you have not
spent your life's energies in vain. To be in that happy
position falls to the lot of very few. Others have had
a stormy passage, but the weather has been fine for
you, and your lucky star has guided you on your
course.

When I was asked to write a book in connexion
with the twenty-fifth anniversary of your first appearance as a conductor, I was in a dilemma, as I've never

done anything of the sort and didn't even know how to set about it. . . . I agreed, however, to do a biographical sketch, with a chronicle of the musical life of our time as its setting, solely because the fifteen years during which we have known each other have bound us together by the memory of so many and so important events, experienced simultaneously, though perhaps in a different way, and for ever unforgettable.

What I have written is not a criticism nor a jubilee offering, but only, as I understand it, the objective testimony of one musician concerning another; the testimony of a friend and contemporary in regard to a period in which we met on a common path and in which we took an active part, each according to his abilities.

Here I stop, dear friend, with my best wishes for your future welfare and for the continuance of your brilliant career in the sphere of art which we cherish. I hope that you will make it possible for someone to write a second book which will tell the story of your achievements in the years between your silver and golden jubilees.

Paris. August 1930

INDEX